Johnny Wei-Bing Lin

A Hands-On Introduction to Using Python in the Atmospheric and Oceanic Sciences

HTTP://WWW.JOHNNY-LIN.COM/PYINTRO

2012

© 2012 Johnny Wei-Bing Lin.
Some rights reserved. Printed version: ISBN 978-1-300-07616-2. PDF versions: No ISBNs are assigned.

This work is licensed under the Creative Commons Attribution-Noncommercial-Share Alike 3.0 United States License (CC BY-NC-SA). To view a copy of this license, visit http://creativecommons.org/licenses/by-nc-sa/3.0/us or send a letter to Creative Commons, 171 Second Street, Suite 300, San Francisco, California, 94105, USA.

Who would *not* want to pay money for this book?: if you do not need a black-and-white paper copy of the book, a color PDF copy with functional hyperlinks, have limited funds, or are interested in such a small portion of the book that it makes no sense to buy the whole thing. The book's web site (http://www.johnny-lin.com/pyintro) has available, for free, PDFs of every chapter as separate files.

Who would want to pay money for this book?: if you want a black-and-white paper copy of the book, a color PDF copy with functional hyperlinks, or you want to help support the author financially. You can buy a black-and-white paper copy of the book at http://www.johnny-lin.com/pyintro/buypaper.shtml and a hyperlink-enabled color PDF copy of the book at http://www.johnny-lin.com/pyintro/buypdf.shtml.

A special appeal to instructors: Instruction at for-profit institutions, as a commercial use, is not covered under the terms of the CC BY-NC-SA, and so instructors at those institutions should not make copies of the book for students beyond copying permitted under Fair Use. Instruction at not-for-profit institutions is not a commercial use, so instructors may legally make copies of this book for the students in their classes, under the terms of the CC BY-NC-SA, so long as no profit is made through the copy and sale (or Fair Use is not exceeded). However, most instruction at not-for-profit institutions still involves payment of tuition: lots of people are getting paid for their contributions. Please consider also paying the author of this book something for his contribution.

Regardless of whether or not you paid money for your copy of the book, you are free to use any and all parts of the book under the terms of the CC BY-NC-SA.

Contents

Preface   v

Notices   xi

How to Use This Book   xiii

1 What Is and Why Python?   1
    1.1 Python: The good and the bad 1
    1.2 Examples of AOS uses for Python 2

2 Using the Python Interpreter and Interactive Development Environment   7
    2.1 Getting and installing Python 7
       2.1.1 The easiest way: EPD 8
       2.1.2 The mostly easy way, but for Ubuntu 12.04 8
       2.1.3 The not as easy way, but it's still free 9
    2.2 Getting and installing the course files 9
    2.3 The Python interpreter 9
    2.4 The command-line environment 11
    2.5 The IDLE environment 12
    2.6 Exercises using Python programming environments 13

3 Basic Data and Control Structures   17
    3.1 Overview of basic variables and operators 17
    3.2 Strings 19
    3.3 Booleans 20
    3.4 NoneType 21
    3.5 Lists and tuples 22
    3.6 Exercises with lists and tuples 25
    3.7 Dictionaries 26
    3.8 Exercises with dictionaries 28

3.9	Functions	29
3.10	Logical constructs	33
3.11	Looping	34
	3.11.1	Looping a definite number of times	34
	3.11.2	Looping an indefinite number of times	36
3.12	Exercises on functions, logical constructs, and looping ...	37
3.13	Modules	39
3.14	A brief introduction to object syntax	41
3.15	Exercise that includes using a module	42
3.16	Exception handling	43
3.17	Summary	45

4 Array Operations   47

4.1	What is an array and the NumPy package	47
4.2	Creating arrays	47
4.3	Array indexing	50
4.4	Exercises in creating and indexing arrays	52
4.5	Array inquiry	53
4.6	Array manipulation	54
4.7	General array operations	58
	4.7.1	General array operations: Method 1 (loops)	58
	4.7.2	General array operations: Method 2 (array syntax)	59
	4.7.3	Exercise on general array operations	62
4.8	Testing inside an array	63
	4.8.1	Testing inside an array: Method 1 (loops)	63
	4.8.2	Testing inside an array: Method 2 (array syntax)	64
	4.8.3	Exercise on testing inside an array	70
4.9	Additional array functions	71
4.10	Summary	72

5 File Input and Output   73

5.1	File objects	74
5.2	Text input/output	74
	5.2.1	Text input/output: Reading a file	75
	5.2.2	Text input/output: Writing a file	75
	5.2.3	Text input/output: Processing file contents	76
	5.2.4	Exercise to read a multi-column text file	79
5.3	NetCDF input/output	79
	5.3.1	NetCDF input/output: Reading a file	80
	5.3.2	NetCDF input/output: Writing a file	84
	5.3.3	Exercise to read and write a netCDF file	86

	5.4	Summary	87

6 A "Real" AOS Project: Putting Together a Basic Data Analysis Routine — 89
- 6.1 The assignment 89
- 6.2 Solution One: Fortran-like structure 90
- 6.3 Solution Two: Store results in arrays 92
- 6.4 Solution Three: Store results in dictionaries 93
- 6.5 Solution Four: Store results and functions in dictionaries . . 94
- 6.6 Exercises on using dictionaries and extending your basic data analysis routine 95
- 6.7 Summary 96

7 An Introduction to OOP Using Python: Part I—Basic Principles and Syntax — 97
- 7.1 What is object-oriented programming 97
  - 7.1.1 Procedural vs. object-oriented programming 98
  - 7.1.2 The nuts and bolts of objects 98
- 7.2 Example of how objects work: Strings 99
- 7.3 Exercise on how objects work: Strings 100
- 7.4 Example of how objects work: Arrays 101
- 7.5 Exercise on how objects work: Arrays 103
- 7.6 Defining your own class 104
- 7.7 Exercise on defining your own class 107
- 7.8 Making classes work together to make complex programming easier 110
- 7.9 Case study 1: The bibliography example 110
  - 7.9.1 Structuring the `Bibliography` class 110
  - 7.9.2 What `sort_entries_alpha` illustrates about OOP . 112
  - 7.9.3 Exercise in extending the `Bibliography` class . . . 113
  - 7.9.4 What the `write_bibliog_alpha` method illustrates about OOP 115
- 7.10 Case study 2: Creating a class for geosciences work—Surface domain management 115
- 7.11 Summary 119

8 An Introduction to OOP Using Python: Part II—Application to Atmospheric Sciences Problems — 121
- 8.1 Managing metadata and missing values 121
  - 8.1.1 What are masked arrays and masked variables? . . . 122
  - 8.1.2 Constructing and deconstructing masked arrays . . . 126

	8.1.3 Exercise using masked arrays	129
8.2	Managing related but unknown data: Seeing if attributes are defined	130
8.3	Exercise to add to the `Atmosphere` class	135
8.4	Dynamically changing subroutine execution order (optional)	137
8.5	Summary	141

9 Visualization: Basic Line and Contour Plots — 143

9.1	What is matplotlib?	143
9.2	Basic line plots	144
	9.2.1 Controlling line and marker formatting	145
	9.2.2 Annotation and adjusting the font size of labels . . .	146
	9.2.3 Plotting multiple figures and curves	150
	9.2.4 Adjusting the plot size	152
	9.2.5 Saving figures to a file	152
9.3	Exercise on basic line plots	153
9.4	Basic contour plots	154
9.5	Exercise on basic contour plots	156
9.6	Superimposing a map	158
9.7	Exercise on superimposing a map	161
9.8	Summary	162

10 What Next? — 165

10.1	What Python topics would be good to cover next?	165
10.2	Some packages of interest to AOS users	167
10.3	Additional references	168
10.4	A parting invitation	169

Glossary — 171

Acronyms — 175

Bibliography — 177

Index — 179

Preface

Why this book and who it is for

There are many good books out there to help people learn the Python programming language but none that I know of that are focused on atmospheric and oceanic sciences (AOS) users. For the highly motivated "early adopter" user, this is not a problem, but for most of us, more general resources are not as useful for two reasons:

- We do not learn programming languages as ends in and of themselves but to help us to better do our AOS work. We are not interested in the nature of object-oriented programming (OOP), but rather we are interested in whether we can use (and how to use) OOP to help us make better model runs, analyze reanalysis data, etc.

- Just because computer scientists are scientists does not mean AOS users will find computer science explanations illuminating. Different disciplines not only speak different languages but they also have different thinking processes. This is even true between the different physical sciences. Thus, learning a language is easier if the explanations and examples are geared to how AOS users think.

This book is a Python introduction for the "rest of us": for researchers, graduate students, and advanced undergraduates who are interested in learning Python but who want to learn first and foremost how Python will help them in their *own* work. The computer science will just come along for the ride.

What we'll cover

I assume that readers will have had some background in procedural programming (perhaps Fortran, IDL, or Matlab) and so already understand variables, arrays, looping, conditionals (if/then), simple input/output, and subroutines/functions. I also assume that in their work, most readers use a procedural programming methodology, writing programs that are broken up into subroutines and functions where input is passed in and out using argument lists (or common blocks or modules). As a result, I start out by showing how you can use Python as a more-or-less drop-in replacement for whatever traditionally procedural programming language you use (e.g., Fortran, IDL, Matlab, etc.). If this is all you want, the first half of the book (Chs. 1–6) should be all you need.

However, while Python can be used solely procedurally,[1] and for many AOS purposes, procedural programming works very well, Python is natively object-oriented, and so users who never tap into Python's object-oriented nature will end up missing one of the key benefits of moving to Python. To put it another way, if you're going to write Fortran code in Python, why not just write it in Fortran? As a result, while the first half of the book (mainly) discusses procedural programming in Python, starting in Ch. 7, I provide a gentle introduction to object-oriented programming and how object-oriented programming can be *applied* to AOS problems to enable us to write analysis and modeling programs that are more reliable, easier to maintain, and enable more science to be done.

Is this the only Python book I'll ever need?

If you're looking to buy and/or use only one Python book, this is not the book for you. If you can learn from a reference book, something like Martelli (2006) would be a great book to use instead of this one: it's comprehensive, concise, authoritative, and clearly written.

When I was learning Python, there was nothing written for a person like me, so I had to use application programming interface (API) documentation, etc. to learn the language. Because I am first an atmospheric scientist, then a programmer, this was very slow going for me. I needed someone to explain to me why Python was structured the way it was, in language that *I* (not a computer scientist) could understand. This is what this book aims to achieve.

After the introduction provided by this book, you should be better able to make full use of reference works like Martelli (2006). In Ch. 10, I provide a list of topics and resources you will want to explore after you finish this book.

---

[1] One of Python's strengths is that it is a multi-paradigm language that can be used procedurally, in an object-oriented way, and/or functionally.

Software you'll need

I assume that you have a (later) version of Python 2.x (preferably 2.7) installed on your computer, along with the NumPy, matplotlib (with Basemap), and ScientificPython packages. Although Python has now moved on to version 3.x, almost all scientific users still use a version of 2.x. Please see Section 2.1 for help on installing Python and the needed packages.

Typesetting and coloring conventions

Throughout the book, I use different forms of typesetting and coloring to provide additional clarity and functionality (text coloring is available in only some versions of the book; later on in this preface I discuss the different versions of the book). Some of the special typesetting conventions I use include:

- Source code: Typeset in a serif, non-proportional font, as in `a = 4`.

- Commands to type on your keyboard or printed to the screen: Typeset in a serif, non-proportional font, as in `print 'hello'`.

- Generic arguments: Typeset in a serif, proportional, italicized font, in between a less than sign and a greater than sign, as in *<condition>*.

- File, directory, and executable names: Typeset in a serif, proportional, italicized font, as in */usr/bin*.

Please note that general references to application, library, module, and package names are not typeset any differently from regular text. Thus, references to the matplotlib package are typeset just as in this sentence. As most packages have unique names, this should not be confusing. In the few cases where the package names are regular English words (e.g., the time module), references to the module will hopefully be clear from the context.

Usually, the first time a key word is used and/or explained, it will be bold in the text **like this.** Key words are found in the glossary, and when useful, occurrences of those words are hyperlinked to the glossary (if the document has hyperlinks). Many acronyms are hyperlinked to the acronym list (again, if the document has hyperlinks). The glossary and acronym lists start on p. 171.

All generic text is in black. All hyperlinks (whether to locations internal or external to the document), if provided, are in blue. All margin notes are in magenta (if the version supports colors).

Updates, additional resources, and versions of this book

Updates and additional resources are available at the book's website, http://www.johnny-lin.com/pyintro. This includes a link to a list of addenda and errata, the latest edition of which you can also access directly by going here: http://www.johnny-lin.com/pyintro/addenda_errata.shtml.

Some of the examples and/or exercises in this book make use of files that are available online for free at the book's website. You'll want to download these files before you start the book; the link to these course files is at the bottom of the book's web page, or you can go directly to http://www.johnny-lin.com/pyintro/course_files.tar (which takes you to the version of these files for the latest edition of the book). In the book, these files are referred to as the files that are found in the *course_files* directory.

There are three versions of the book available. While the textual content is the same in all of them, you should know about the differences, so you can find the one that works for you:

- Print version: Black-and-white text and margin notes; black-and-white figures; no hyperlinks; all chapters bound together; margins formatted for binding; includes a cover; costs money.

- Full PDF version: Black-and-white text and colored margin notes; color figures; colored and enabled hyperlinks; all chapters in a single file; margins formatted without binding; includes a cover; costs money.

- Free PDF version: Black-and-white text and colored margin notes; color figures; no hyperlinks; each chapter in a separate file; margins formatted without binding; does not include a cover; available for free at the book's website.

Although the PDF versions are not bound, the pagination and the formatting are kept consistent with the printed version, i.e., the same paper size and as if printed on left-right opening two-sided pages. Thus, all text, figures, and notes will be in the same relative places on the page, whether it is PDF or printed; the only difference is that with the PDF versions the margins are different to reflect the lack of a binding offset.

Information on how to obtain each version of the book is found on the copyright page (the page right after the title page). Links to access all versions of the book are also given at the book's website, http://www.johnny-lin.com/pyintro. Note, as a special gift for purchasing the printed version, the original owners of a print copy of this book can download a copy of the latest edition of the Full PDF version of the book for free. Please see the last page of the printed book (the Colophon page) for details.

Personal Acknowledgments

While I often use first person throughout this book, I am acutely aware of the debt I owe to family, friends, and colleagues who, over many years, generously nurtured many of the ideas in this book: Indeed, we all do stand on the shoulders of giants, as Newton said. All praise I happily yield to them; any mistakes and errors are my own.

Much of this book came from a series of short courses I taught at the 2011 and 2012 American Meteorological Society (AMS) Annual Meetings. I want to thank Charles Doutriaux and Dean Williams who were co-teachers in those courses and my students from those courses whose questions and comments helped refine my teaching of this material.

Interactions with and/or support of the following are very much appreciated: Nick Barnes, Dan Braithwaite, Dave Brown, Rodrigo Caballero, June Chang, Laura Clemente, Christian Dieterich, Tyler Erickson, Chih-Yung Feng, Mike Fiorino, Zech Gelzer, Mary Haley, Rob Jacob, Linda McDonald, Tim Olusanya, Ray Pierrehumbert, Ricky Rood, Mike Steder, and Kirsten Trout.

Thanks too for ideas and reference assistance from: Yun-Lan Chen and her colleagues at the Central Weather Bureau (Taiwan) and PyAOS commenter "N eil"[2] (Ch. 6); Peter Caldwell (Ch. 8); Mary Haley and the online and/or interpreter PyNGL, matplotlib, and Basemap documentation (Ch. 9); and the online and/or interpreter Python, NumPy, and CDAT documentation (multiple chapters of the book).

I am personally grateful for those who gave me permission to use material they created: These are acknowledged in the Notices section starting on p. xi and in the captions of the included or adapted figures. And my overflowing thanks to those who provided feedback on drafts of the book: Yun-Lan Chen and her colleagues at the Central Weather Bureau, Taiwan, Alex Decaria, Karen Lin, Grant Petty, and Scott Sellars.

---

[2]See the first comment on http://pyaos.johnny-lin.com/?p=755 (accessed August 16, 2012).

The Real Reason Newton Couldn't Solve the Three Body Problem

My father and mother, sister Joann and brother-in-law Cary, and nephew and niece Tyler and Claire, have given me so much of themselves over the years. My sons Timothy and James fill my life with their infectious laughter (the above comic is firmly tongue-in-cheek ☺), and my wife Karen's love and partnership with me in this book is beyond praise. I started working at home on this book, in earnest, the same week we began to toilet train our eldest son; that alone says volumes about how sacrificially she has supported me in bringing this book to fruition. Finally, I thank my Lord and Savior Jesus Christ for giving me the one fundamental prerequisite for writing this book, life itself, both physically and spiritually: "... I have come that they may have life, and have it to the full" (John 10:10b, NIV).

Johnny Wei-Bing Lin
Chicago, Illinois
August 18, 2012

Notices

Trademark Acknowledgments

ArcGIS is a registered trademark of Environmental Systems Research Institute, Inc. Debian is a registered trademark of Software in the Public Interest, Inc. IDL is a registered trademark of Exelis Corporation. Linux is a trademark owned by Linus Torvalds. Mac, Mac OS, and OS X are registered trademarks of Apple Inc. Mathematica is a trademark of Wolfram Research, Inc. Matlab and MathWorks are registered trademarks of The MathWorks, Inc. Perl is a registered trademark of Yet Another Society. Python is a registered trademark of the Python Software Foundation. Solaris is a trademark of Oracle. Swiss Army is a registered trademark of Victorinox AG, Ibach, Switzerland and its related companies. Ubuntu is a registered trademark of Canonical Ltd. Windows is a registered trademark of Microsoft Corporation. All other marks mentioned in this book are the property of their respective owners. Any errors or omissions in trademark and/or other mark attribution are not meant to be assertions of trademark and/or other mark rights.

Copyright Acknowledgments

Scripture taken from the HOLY BIBLE, NEW INTERNATIONAL VERSION®. Copyright © 1973, 1978, 1984 Biblica. Used by permission of Zondervan. All rights reserved. The "NIV" and "New International Version" trademarks are registered in the United States Patent and Trademark Office by Biblica. Use of either trademark requires the permission of Biblica.

Portions of Ch. 1 are taken and/or adapted from Lin (2012), © Copyright 2012 American Meteorological Society (AMS) and are used by permission. Permission to use figures, tables, and brief excerpts from Lin (2012) in scientific and educational works is hereby granted provided that the source is acknowledged. Any use of material in Lin (2012) that is determined to be "fair use" under Section 107 of the U.S. Copyright Act or that satisfies the conditions specified in Section 108 of the U.S. Copyright Act (17 USC §108, as revised by P.L. 94-553) does not require the AMS's permission. Republication, systematic reproduction, posting in electronic form, such as on a web site or in a searchable database, or other uses of Lin (2012), except as exempted by the above statement, requires written permission or a license from the AMS. Additional details are provided in the AMS Copyright Policy, available on the AMS Web site located at http://www.ametsoc.org or from the AMS at 617-227-2425 or copyright@ametsoc.org. Lin (2012) has been submitted for publication and thus copyright in that work may be transferred without further notice, and that version may no longer be accessible.

Sprinkled throughout the book are comics from *Under the Microscope*, a whimsical look at the world of geoscience, academia, and the meaning of life, by Dan Johnson and Johnny Lin, and are used by permission. The comics are available online at http://www.johnny-lin.com/comic. In some cases, the comics I've included are related to the section at hand; in others, they're just for fun.

All figures not created by myself are used by permission and are noted either in this acknowledgments section or in the respective figure captions. Use in this book of information from all other resources is believed to be covered under Fair Use doctrine.

Other Usage Acknowledgments

The cover image (if a cover is provided) was resized and cropped from an image taken by the crew of Expedition 23 on-board the International Space Station (ISS) on May 25, 2010 and shows an edge-on view of the Earth's atmosphere over the Indian Ocean (outer space is to the upper right). The image is provided by the ISS Crew Earth Observations experiment and Image Science and Analysis Laboratory, at NASA's Johnson Space Center. The image is available online at http://earthobservatory.nasa.gov/IOTD/view.php?id=44267 and is not copyrighted.

The dataset of monthly mean surface/near-surface air temperature from the NCEP/NCAR Reanalysis 1 was taken from NCEP Reanalysis data provided by the NOAA/OAR/ESRL PSD, Boulder, Colorado, USA from their web site at http://www.esrl.noaa.gov/psd.

How to Use This Book

First, the bad news: How not to use this book

Because I wrote this book to help teach atmospheric and oceanic scientists brand-new to Python how to use the language, there are a lot of things the book does not do well, and there are a lot of topics the book does not cover.

Things the book does not do well: This book is a bad Python reference. The order in the book matters, because the topics build on each another. This book also does a poor job of telling you how to install Python. I touch on it in Section 2.1, but that isn't the focus of the book.

Topics that are not covered: This book is geared for beginners so I had to leave out a lot of topics that, while important, are not central to helping beginners use *and* understand Python. Topics I have left out include: object inheritance, operating system commands, environment customization, wrapping Fortran routines, and many worthy visualization packages. I describe some of these topics in Section 10.1, but only enough to motivate the reader to look into those issues after they have a handle on the concepts I do cover.

How not to use the book: Along the lines of using this book as a reference, you will find the book to be sorely lacking if you ignore the exercises. Yes, every author says "do the exercises," but in this book, the exercises are intimately interwoven with the pedagogy. Skipping the exercises is not just skipping breakfast, but more like skipping air. (I talk about this more below.)

How to use this book

I recommend you don't think of this book as a text you're reading but as a course you're taking. (In fact, the source code and sample data files are in a directory called *course_files* and much of the content comes from the 2012 AMS Annual Meeting Beginner's Python short course I taught.) As a course you're taking (either a self-study course or a course with an instructor), this will involve not just reading but a lot of doing.

I am a firm believer that the only real way you can learn a programming language is to program in that language—this book has "hands-on" in its title for a reason ☺. As a result, this book is built around examples and exercises for the reader. I will start off by discussing a topic, and interspersed with that discussion will be worked out examples of varying degrees of complexity. *You really have to type in the examples,* even if they are worked out and explained in the text; otherwise, you won't get much out of the text. After discussion and examples, I provide exercises that implement the material we just discussed. *Those exercises are also crucial to getting the most out of the book.* In fact, for a number of the exercises, later discussion builds off of your attempt (successful or not) at completing the exercise.[3]

All examples and exercises are numbered globally; numbering does not restart with a new chapter.

Before you start using the book, you'll want to download the supporting files for some of the examples and exercises. In the book, these will the files referred to as residing in the directory *course_files*. This directory of files is available online at the book's website; see p. viii for details on how to obtain the files.

Additional notes about the way I wrote this book

Tone: Because I grew up in Seattle and did my undergraduate and graduate work all in California, I'm a "son of the West" (to misappropriate Tolkien's phrase), and so I've written this book in a more informal, conversational tone. (I use contractions and put in smileys ☺.) I hope you find my voice to be something of a "tour guide" of Python and that you will be encouraged to explore and try things out. Ultimately, I think this will make it both easier to learn Python and more fun.

Repetition: In most academic papers and books, the author will talk about a topic once and then (often) assume you remember what was said for the rest of this book. I always found it frustrating when textbook authors followed that convention. Repetition is one of the best ways to teach (and learn); why don't textbook authors take advantage of this pedagogy? Besides, if I am a brand-new learner, I probably will not fully understand a concept the first time I hear it. Thus, in this book, I repeat myself, repeatedly. If you are a naturally gifted programmer, you may find this annoying, and I apologize for annoying you, but then again, I didn't write this book for naturally

---

[3]This pedagogy is based on an AMS Board on Continuing Professional Development template derived from a template by Results Through Training <http://www.RTTWorks.com>.

Chapter	Subject	Class Hours
1	What Is and Why Python	1
2	Using the Python Interpreter and Interactive Development Environment	1
3	Basic Data and Control Structures	3
4	Array Operations	3
5	File Input and Output	2
6	A "Real" AOS Project: Putting Together a Basic Data Analysis Routine	1
7	An Introduction to OOP Using Python: Part I—Basic Principles and Syntax	3
8	An Introduction to OOP Using Python: Part II—Application to Atmospheric Sciences Problems	2
9	Visualization: Basic Line and Contour Plots	3
10	What Next?	1

Table 1: Breakdown of class time to cover each chapter.

gifted programmers but for people like myself who learned programming by looping through the topic many times.

A note to instructors

As I mentioned earlier, this book works well for self-study but can also be used as part of a course. When I taught this as short course, we covered nearly 80% of the material over the course of two (long) days. Table 1 gives an estimate of how much class time each chapter will take, in instructor contact hours. This totals 20 class hours. Depending on whether and how you augment the content with additional homework exercises and projects, this book will work for a 2 credit hour, one quarter (10 week) class or a 1–2 credit hour, one semester (15 week) class.

The AMS 2012 Short Courses web page has PDF copies of the presentation slides for the Beginner's course as well as an Advanced course that was also offered. You're welcome to download and use the slides under the terms of their license: please see http://pyaos.johnny-lin.com/?page_id=807.

An online, introductory Python course

If you're interested in an online, introductory, AOS Python course taught by the author of this book, please email me at pyintro@johnny-lin.com. The course includes real-time, interactive video lectures (which can also be viewed outside of the scheduled class meeting time), not just online assignments and interaction.

Chapter 1

What Is and Why Python?

1.1 Python: The good and the bad

So, what's with all the fuss about Python? If you're reading this book, you might have heard about Python from a co-worker who swears by it, heard a reference to the language in a talk at a conference, or followed a link from a page on scientific computing. When you've asked others about Python, they might have thrown out words like "object-oriented," "interpreted," or "open-source." What does all this mean?

This book answers that question, from the standpoint of a researcher in the atmospheric or oceanic sciences. That doesn't mean, however, there isn't a shorter answer to the question. Here is one summary list of the attributes and features of Python:

- Structure: Python is a **multi-paradigm language**, and can be used for scripting, **procedural programming**, as a fully native object-oriented (OO) language, and as a functional language.

- Interpreted: Python is loosely or **dynamically typed** and interactive. There is no separate compiler but rather commands typed into the interpreter are automatically compiled, linked (as needed) and executed.

- Data structures: Python has a robust built-in set of data types, and users are free to define additional structures.

- Syntax: Easy to read and includes an array syntax that is similar to Matlab, IDL, and Fortran 90 (no loops!).

- Platform independent, open-source, and *free!*

But what do these features allow you to do? Here is where Python users start waxing enthusiastically. First, because of Python's concise but natural syntax, for both arrays and non-arrays, programs are exceedingly clear and easy to read; as the saying goes, "Python is executable pseudocode. Perl is executable line noise."[1] Second, because the language is interpreted, development is much easier; you do not have to spend extra time with manipulating a compiler and linker. Third, the object-orientation makes code more robust/less brittle, and the built-in set of data structures are very powerful and useful (e.g., dictionaries). Fourth, Python is designed with a built-in namespace management structure which naturally prevents variable and function collisions. In contrast with linking multiple Fortran libraries, where you can easily overwrite a function from one library with a function from another, in Python you have to work at causing such a collision. Finally, Python's open-source pedigree added with a large user and developer base in industry, as well as science—institutions supporting AOS Python include Lawrence Livermore National Laboratory (LLNL)'s Program for Coupled Model Diagnostics and Intercomparison (PCMDI) and National Center for Atmospheric Research (NCAR)'s Computational Information Systems Laboratory (CISL)—means that your programs can take advantage of the tens of thousands of Python **packages** that exist. Multiple visualization packages are available, some numerical libraries, packages that deliver tight interconnects with compiled languages (Fortran via f2py and C via SWIG), memory caching, webservices, graphical user interface (GUI) programming, etc. You are not limited to only what one vendor can provide, or even what only the scientific community can provide!

To be fair, Python has real disadvantages, including that pure Python code runs much slower than compiled code, there are comparatively few scientific libraries compared to Fortran, and documentation and support for new science users is relatively sparse. There are tools to overcome the speed penalty, the collection of scientific libraries is growing, and science support resources are becoming more robust (which this book hopefully contributes to), but these are real issues. For many, if not most, AOS applications, however, the strengths of Python outweigh the weaknesses.

1.2 Examples of AOS uses for Python

But this all sounds kind of abstract: what are some examples of what Python can do for AOS users? Figure 1.1 shows examples of typical AOS visual-

---

[1] I don't know who first said this, but you can find one instance of this quote at http://mindview.net/Books/Python/ThinkingInPython.html (accessed March 14, 2012).

ization tasks (skew-T and meteograms), using the PyNGL package, which implements all the primitives (and some of the higher-level functions) of the NCAR Graphics Language (NGL). Figure 1.2 shows screenshots of an application (WxMAP2) written in Python that visualizes and delivers weather maps of numerical weather prediction model results. And Figure 1.3 shows an application written in Python (VisTrails) that manages provenance in the context of geoscientific analysis and visualization: VisTrails enables you to analyze and visualize a dataset while at the same time keeping a record of the operations you did. As these examples show, Python can be used for nearly any analysis and visualization task you would want to do in AOS research and operations.

When Meteorologists Play With Their Food

As neat as these examples are, however, the greatest advantage of Python to AOS work (in my opinion) is how it enables one to have a truly unified workflow: analysis, visualization, and workflow management are all (potentially) integrated together. Figure 1.4 illustrates this potential. As shown in the figure, the problem encountered by the Northeast Regional Climate Center (NRCC) was how to unify the many different components of the Applied Climate Information System: data ingest, distribution, storage, analysis, web services (tasks and formats in black). The traditional solution would be to cobble together a crazy mix of shell scripts, compiled code, makefiles, Matlab/IDL scripts, and a web server. (And when you think of it, most AOS workflows are like that; a crazy mix of tools that talk to each other through

Python enables a unified workflow.

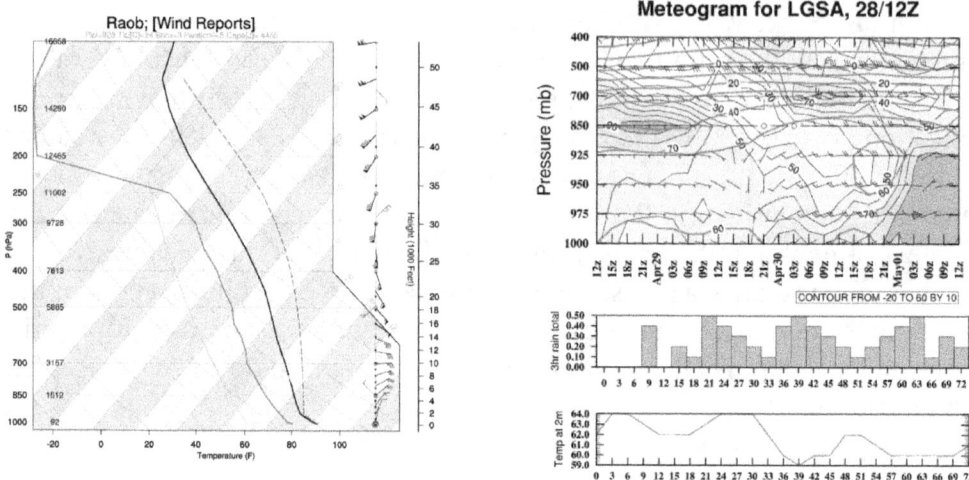

Figure 1.1: Visualization of a skew-T plot and a meteogram using PyNGL. These plots are taken from the PyNGL website http://www.pyngl.ucar.edu. See http://www.pyngl.ucar.edu/Examples/gallery.shtml for the source code to make the plots. Plots are copyright, University Corporation for Atmospheric Research. Graphics were generated with PyNGL, developed at NCAR and sponsored by NSF. Used by permission.

text pipes or files.) NRCC's solution: Do it all in Python (package names in red), and the resulting single environment of shared state created a more powerful, flexible, and maintainable system than would otherwise have been possible.

So, this is why I'm so excited about Python and why I wrote this book! Python is a flexible, powerful, open, and free language whose native object-oriented structure permits more robust programs to be written. The result is a language that enables better atmospheric and oceanic sciences to be done more easily at less cost, both in time and money. The bottom line is that Python enables me to do my science more easily and reliably; how cool is that?

1.2. EXAMPLES OF AOS USES FOR PYTHON

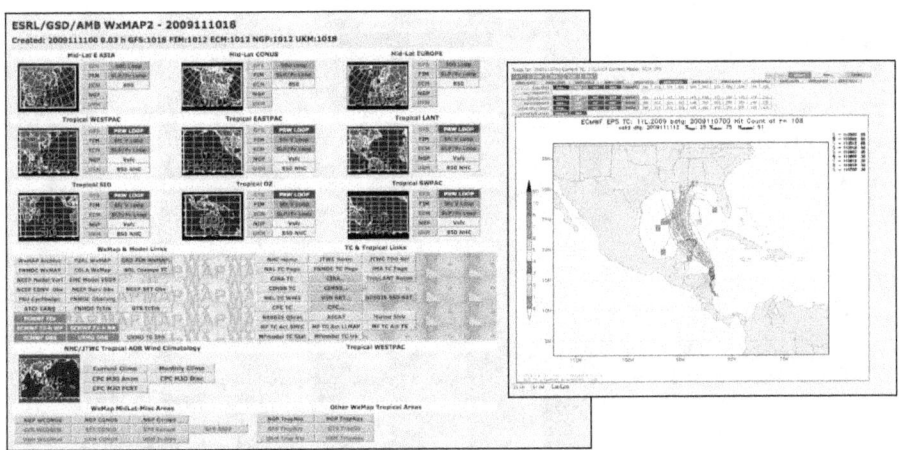

Figure 1.2: Screenshots taken from the WxMAP2 package web site. See: http://sourceforge.net/projects/wxmap2. These screenshots are by Michael Fiorino (NOAA Earth System Research Laboratory, Boulder, CO.) and are used by permission.

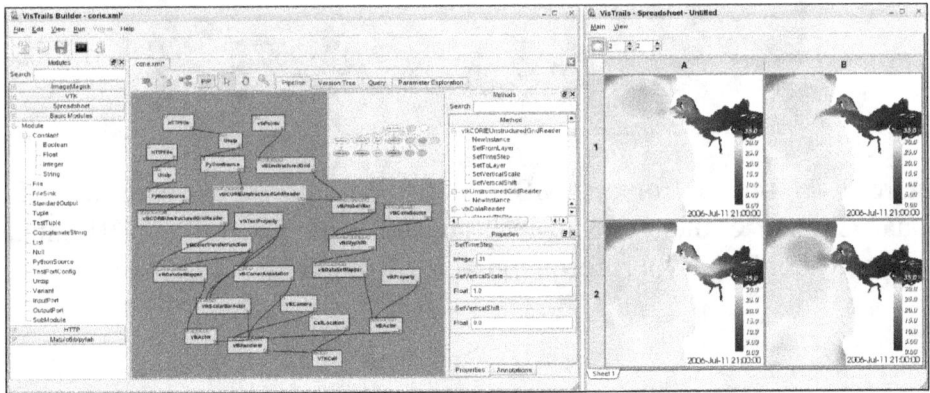

Figure 1.3: Session of the VisTrails visualization and data workflow and provenance management system; salinity data in the Columbia River estuary is graphed. See: http://www.vistrails.org/index.php?title=File:Corie_example.png&oldid=616. The screenshot is by Steven Callahan and is used by permission.

1.2. EXAMPLES OF AOS USES FOR PYTHON

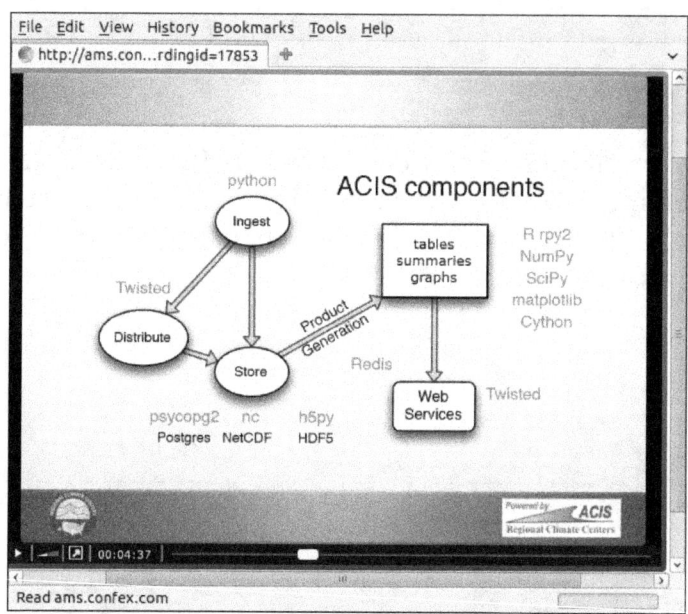

Figure 1.4: Image from: AMS talk by William Noon, Northeast Regional Climate Center, Ithaca, NY, http://ams.confex.com/ams/91Annual/flvgateway.cgi/id/17853?recordingid=17853. Used by permission.

Chapter 2

Using the Python Interpreter and Interactive Development Environment

2.1 Getting and installing Python

In Ch. 1, we saw how Python is practically the best thing for AOS users since sliced bread ☺. Now that I've built-up your expectations, I need to describe the first place where things are not all they should be in the Python universe, and that is the level of support for installation and new science users. In contrast with commercial data analysis software companies (e.g., MathWorks, Wolfram Research, etc.), which make installation a piece-of-cake and provide copious amounts of online, print, and live-human support, installation of Python and all the libraries needed by science users can be tricky. And once the install is complete, there is no simple and comprehensive way to find out everything you have and how to use it.

So, if you're a newbie, what do you do? Unfortunately, there are many ways to install Python and the needed scientific libraries. In this section, I will describe three different ways: just choose the one that works best for you. Each has its pluses and minuses. The first two do not require you to be a budding system administrator (though you will need the password of a user with administrator privileges). The last one requires you to build something from source, so that installation method is for those who are willing to experiment a little more. Please pay attention to the footnotes in this section; that's where I'll put the addresses to the web pages you'll want to access.

2.1. GETTING AND INSTALLING PYTHON

2.1.1 The easiest way: EPD

EPD is the easiest way to install Python and the needed scientific libraries.

The easiest way to get Python is to install the Enthought Python Distribution (EPD),[1] which bundles Python with over 100 modules and packages in an easy to install package. The full distribution is free to employees and students of academic institutions.[2] Commercial users have to pay money. Once you have EPD installed, you will have both Python and all the libraries you need to do all the examples and exercises in this book; see Enthought's "Getting Started with EPD" instructions for information on running EPD once you have it installed.[3] EPD is available for Mac OS X, Windows, GNU/Linux, and Solaris.

Enthought also offers a stripped down version of EPD, free to everyone (not just those in academia), called EPD Free.[4] EPD Free is enough to do most of the examples and exercises in this book, except for the overlaying of continental boundary maps on matplotlib plots. In this book, I use the Basemap package to plot those boundaries, and Basemap is not included with EPD Free (though Basemap is included with the full EPD).

If you already have EPD Free and you want to install Basemap, you can use Enthought's package manager to do so: just type `enpkg basemap` at the command-line.[5] However, you need to have an EPD subscription in order to use enpkg; that subscription costs money.[6]

2.1.2 The mostly easy way, but for Ubuntu 12.04

Installing using a package manager on Ubuntu 12.04.

With the Ubuntu 12.04 GNU/Linux distribution (and perhaps later versions), the standard **package manager** will enable you to install everything you need to run Python and do all the examples and exercises in this book.[7] Log in as a user with administrator privileges, open a terminal window, and type in the following at the Unix command-line:

---

[1] http://www.enthought.com/products/epd.php (accessed August 16, 2012).

[2] The academic download is accessed on this page: http://www.enthought.com/products/edudownload.php (accessed August 16, 2012).

[3] http://www.enthought.com/products/epdgetstart.php (accessed August 16, 2012).

[4] http://www.enthought.com/products/epd_free.php (accessed August 16, 2012).

[5] http://www.enthought.com/products/update.php (accessed August 16, 2012).

[6] http://www.enthought.com/products/getepd.php (accessed August 16, 2012).

[7] See http://packages.ubuntu.com/precise/python for a list of Python packages on Ubuntu 12.04 (accessed August 16, 2012).

```
sudo apt-get update
sudo apt-get install python2.7
sudo apt-get install python-matplotlib
sudo apt-get install python-scipy
sudo apt-get install python-scientific
sudo apt-get install python-mpltoolkits.basemap
```

Feel free to substitute in your favorite package manager (I actually use aptitude instead) for apt-get. After these commands are run, you will have Python 2.7 (plus select libraries) installed.

2.1.3 The not as easy way, but it's still free

If you aren't running Ubuntu 12.04, but you are using Mac OS X or another version of GNU/Linux, you can still use a package manager to install Python and most of the needed scientific packages for this book and build the final package needed (Basemap) from source. See the PyAOS articles on installing on a Mac[8] and installing on GNU/Linux[9] for details. (Note these articles address an installation using Python 2.5; the names may have changed for Python 2.7 related packages.)

While Python works fine on Windows, for the rest of this book, I will assume that you are using a Unix system (e.g., Mac OS X, GNU/Linux, etc.). For many operating systems, the default distribution of Python and associated applications are located in /usr/bin; if your system is different, please substitute accordingly anytime you see /usr/bin in this book.

2.2 Getting and installing the course files

Throughout this book, you will find reference to files from a directory called *course_files*. This directory of files is not part of a Python distribution but is instead a set of files I have created for this book. This directory of files is available online at the book's website; see p. viii for details on accessing the site and files.

2.3 The Python interpreter

Python is an interpreted language, meaning that you just type in a command in Python, press Enter, and Python will execute that command right then and

---

[8]http://pyaos.johnny-lin.com/?p=190 (accessed August 16, 2012).
[9]http://pyaos.johnny-lin.com/?p=76 (accessed August 16, 2012).

2.3. THE PYTHON INTERPRETER

there. This is similar to the behavior of Matlab, IDL, and Mathematica, and the environment where this all occurs in Python is called the **interpreter**. Let's try an example:

Example 1 (My first Python interpreter command):

Start out by opening a **terminal window**. Everything you do will be in that window.

- Start the Python interpreter by typing `python` at the Unix command-line. You should get something that looks like Figure 2.1. If this doesn't happen, here are some possible fixes:

    Questions to ask if you can't start the Python interpreter.

    – If your environment path is not set up correctly, you may have to type in the full path name to your Python binary. One common name is `/usr/bin/python`.

    – On some other installations, you may have to type in the version of Python you want, e.g., `python2.5`.

    – If you are using Mac OS X and you installed Python using EPD, you may have to type something like:

    `/Library/Frameworks/Python.Framework/Versions/7.3/bin/python`

    instead of just `python` (or you may want to add the EPD Python path to your shell environment's *PATH* variable).

    – If you are using Mac OS X and you installed Python using the Fink package manager, you may have to type something like `/sw/bin/python2.5`.

- When you see the >>> prompt, type:

    `print "hello world!"`

    and press Enter.

- The interpreter immediately executes the command, printing the string `hello world!` to screen.

- To exit the interpreter and return to the Unix command-line, type Ctrl-d.

Press Ctrl-d to exit the interpreter.

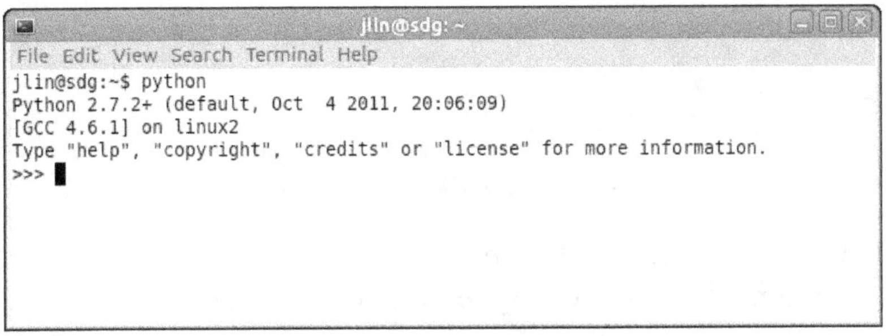

[Figure: screenshot of terminal window showing Python interpreter startup]

Figure 2.1: Starting the Python interpreter in a terminal window.

The Python interpreter has two very helpful interpreter commands:

- `help(x)`: This shows online help for the command x.

- `dir()`: This shows (approximately) all the variables and functions defined in the current scope.

The `help` and `dir` commands.

We'll talk more about these commands as we go along. For now, just keep them in mind.

Usually, you will write code in a file and ask Python to execute the code, rather than doing everything interactively in the interpreter. There are a number of excellent and sophisticated programming (or development) environments available for Python, such as IPython,[10] Python(x,y),[11] and Spyder.[12] For our purposes, we'll go basic and consider two very simple ways of setting up a programming environment.

Other development environments for Python.

2.4 The command-line environment

In this example, we set up a programming environment using multiple terminal windows.

Example 2 (A simple command-line programming environment):

- Open two terminal windows on your desktop.

- In one window, use a text editor (e.g., vim, emacs, gedit) to open a file *foo.py*.

---

[10] http://ipython.scipy.org (accessed August 16, 2012).
[11] http://code.google.com/p/pythonxy (accessed August 16, 2012).
[12] http://packages.python.org/spyder (accessed August 16, 2012).

- In that file, type: `print "hello world!"`
- Save the file.
- In the other window, type: `python -i foo.py`
- Python will execute the commands in your file and leave you in the interpreter, where you can type in more commands, if you wish.

The -i option; interpreter command history.

Note, to automatically exit to the operating system after executing the Python commands in your file, do not include the `-i` option.

An aside regarding command history: On many Unix systems, the up- and down-arrow keys allow you to scroll through the history of the commands typed into the interpreter, with the up-arrow scrolling into the past and the down-arrow scrolling back towards the present. This feature, however, is a function of how readline is implemented in the operating system, so this may or may not work for you.

2.5 The IDLE environment

Python comes with its own interactive **development environment** called IDLE. IDLE is actually written in Python, using the Tk GUI widgets system.

Example 3 (Using IDLE):

- To start IDLE, at the command-line, type: `idle &`
  - The ampersand puts the process in the background.
  - If you are using Mac OS X, you may have to first start up X11.
  - Sometimes you have to specify the version number of IDLE, e.g., `idle2.5`. On Ubuntu, it might be called `idle-python2.7`, or something similar.

IDLE has a source code window and a shell window.

- A Python Shell window will automatically open up. (You should get something like what is shown in Figure 2.2, though yours will probably be a little larger.) This window contains a Python interpreter (shown by the >>> prompt), and so whenever in this book I talk about typing something into the interpreter, if it's short, you can type it in here.

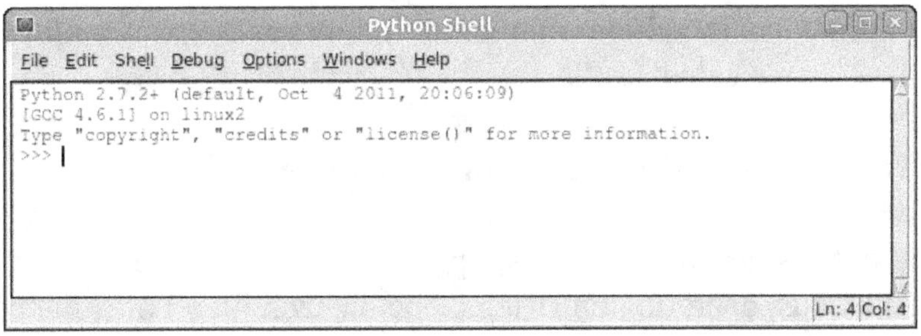

Figure 2.2: The Python shell in IDLE, just started.

- In the menu bar of the Python Shell window, pick File → New Window. (This is a window for a code file. Whenever in this book I talk about typing something into the interpreter, and it's long, type it in here, save it, and run it as described in the next few bullet points.)

- In that window, type: `print "hello world!"`

- Save the file as *foo.py* using File → Save.

- In that same window (your code window), pick Run → Run Module.

- Python will execute, in the Python Shell window, the commands you typed in your code file.

An aside regarding command history: In IDLE, the up- and down-arrows generally do not work to access command history. Instead, place the mouse on the line of the Python Shell you want to execute again, click on that line (i.e., click on the left mouse button; do not select or highlight the line), then press Return, and the line will be duplicated at the current interpreter cursor. If you press Return again, that line will be executed.

Command history in IDLE.

2.6 Exercises using Python programming environments

Exercises are your opportunity to implement what you've learned by trying out the examples; usually, exercises are permutations of topics you've seen in the examples. Try the following exercises to help you get used to the

2.6. EXERCISES USING PYTHON PROGRAMMING ENVIRONMENTS

command-line and IDLE environments. Exercise 2 also introduces using Python as a simple calculator.

▷ **Exercise 1 (Printing some words to the screen):**

The print command.

- In your first terminal window, open a file and type in a series of `print` commands, operating on strings, one on each line. For instance:

```
print "My name is Johnny Lin."
print "I think Python is neat."
print "I wish I had used it for my Ph.D."
```

- Save the file.

- In your second terminal window, run the file. Did you get what you expected?

- Change one of the lines and add another line printing additional text. Save the file and re-run it.

▷ **Exercise 2 (Using Python as a simple calculator):**

Python as a calculator.

- In your first terminal window, open a file and type in a series of `print` commands, with an arithmetic calculation expression as the argument, one on each line. For instance:

```
print 5*4
print 6/2
print 13+5+7
print 6**2
```

- Save the file. Predict what will happen when you run the file.

- In your second terminal window, run the file. Did you get what you predicted?

- Change one of the lines in the file, save the file, and re-run it.

2.6. EXERCISES USING PYTHON PROGRAMMING ENVIRONMENTS

Solution and discussion: (Cover this up if you haven't finished the exercise!) We'll be talking more about this in Ch. 3, but if you typed in a case where you divided two integers, and the division was not even, you might have encountered results you did not expect. For integer division, when the two operands are both integers, Python throws away the remainder and returns only the quotient.

Integer division discards the remainder.

▷ **Exercise 3 (Getting used to the IDLE environment):**
Do Exercises 1 and 2, but using the IDLE environment.

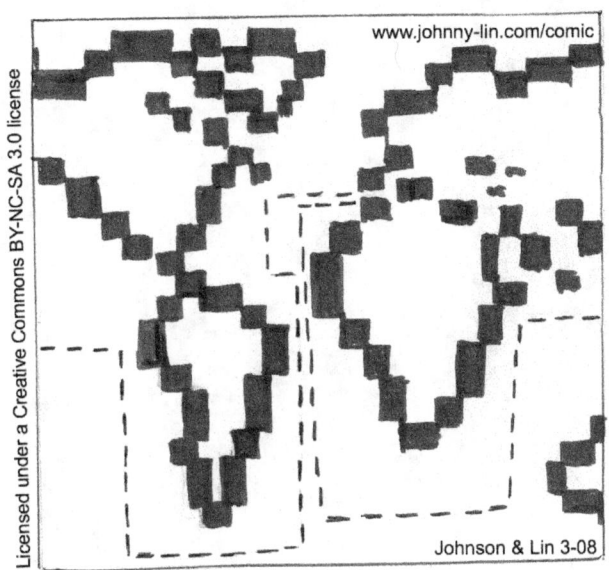

Magellan Circumnavigates the World: A GCM Study

2.6. EXERCISES USING PYTHON PROGRAMMING ENVIRONMENTS

Chapter 3

Basic Data and Control Structures

Python, like any other programming language, has variables and all the standard control structures. As a multi-paradigm language, however, Python has data and control structures not commonly found in languages traditionally used by AOS users. In this chapter, I will describe Python's basic data and control structures that support procedural programming. By the end of this chapter, you should be able to write Fortran programs in Python ☺.

3.1 Overview of basic variables and operators

Unlike languages like Fortran, Python is dynamically typed, meaning that variables take on the type of whatever they are set to when they are assigned. Thus, a=5 makes the variable a an integer, but a=5.0 makes the variable a a floating point number. Additionally, because assignment can happen anytime during the program, this means you can change the type of the variable without changing the variable name.

Python is dynamically typed.

The built-in variable types are as you would guess, along with a few others. Here's a partial list of some of the most important basic types:

- Integer (short and long) and floating point (float)

- Strings

- Booleans

- NoneType

- Lists and tuples

- Dictionaries

3.1. OVERVIEW OF BASIC VARIABLES AND OPERATORS

The first three items are probably familiar to you, but NoneType, lists, tuples, and dictionaries might not be. I'll be talking about all these types as we go along in this chapter.

Arithmetic and comparison operators. Arithmetic operators are as you would guess: (+, -, /, *, ** for addition, subtraction, division, multiplication, and exponentiation, respectively), as are comparison operators (>, <, >=, <=, !=, == for greater than, less than, greater than or equal to, less than or equal to, not equal, and equal, respectively).

Python is case-sensitive. Please note that Python is case-sensitive, so "N" and "n" are different.

Example 4 (Create and use some numerical variables):

Open up a Python interpreter by typing `python` in a terminal window or use the Python Shell in IDLE. Type these lines in in the interpreter:

```
a = 3.5
b = -2.1
c = 3
d = 4
a*b
b+c
a/c
c/d
```

What did you find?

Solution and discussion: You should have gotten something like this:

```
>>> a = 3.5
>>> b = -2.1
>>> c = 3
>>> d = 4
>>> a*b
-7.3500000000000005
>>> b+c
0.8999999999999999
>>> a/c
1.1666666666666667
>>> c/d
0
```

Remember Python is dynamically typed: It automatically decides what type a variable is based on the value/operation. Thus, a and b are floats and c and d are integers.

For operations, Python will generally make the output type the type that retains the most information. E.g., if one of the variables is float, a float variable is returned. However, if both variables are integers, integer division is performed, where the remainder is discarded. Thus a/c returns what you expect since a is float, but c/d does integer division and returns only the quotient (as an integer). Note that in Python 2.x, integers can be short or long; short has a size limit but long does not. In Python 3.x, all integers are long.

Python usually upcasts type if needed.

Here's a question: Why is the answer to a*b not exactly −7.35? Remember that floating point numbers on any binary computer are, in general, not represented exactly.[1] (This is why you should never do logical equality comparisons between floating point numbers; instead, you should compare whether two floating point numbers are "close to" each other. The NumPy array package has a function `allclose` that does this.) The default formatting setting for the `print` command, will sometimes print out enough of the portion after the decimal point to show that.

Binary floating point representations are inexact and the `allclose` function.

Let's take a look in more detail at the non-numeric built-in data types I listed before, i.e., strings, booleans, NoneType, lists and tuples, and dictionaries.

3.2 Strings

String variables are created by setting text in either paired single or double quotes (it doesn't normally matter which, as long as they are consistently paired), e.g.: a = `"hello"`.

Creating strings.

Some "special" strings include:

Special strings.

- `"\n"`: **newline character**

- `"\t"`: tab character

- `"\\"`: backslash

---

[1] See Bruce Bush's article "The Perils of Floating Point," http://www.lahey.com/float.htm (accessed March 17, 2012).

Triple quotes. Python has a special construct called "triple quotes," i.e., quotation marks or apostrophes placed one after the other ("""), which delimit strings that are set to whatever is typed in between the triple quotes, (more or less) verbatim. This includes newline characters (but not backslashes), so this is an easy way to make strings with complex formatting.

Connecting strings. Finally, Python uses the addition operator (+) to join strings together.

Example 5 (An operation with strings):
Try typing this in a Python interpreter:

```
a = "hello"
b = "there"
a + b
```

What did you get? Also try: `print a + b`.

Solution and discussion: The first two lines set `a` and `b` as string variables with values set to the given strings. Because the addition sign concatenates two strings together, `a + b` will return the string `'hellothere'`. The `print` command gives you the same thing, but it does not include the quotes which show that the result of `a + b` is a string.

3.3 Booleans

Boolean variables are variables that can have only one of two values, one of which is considered "true" and the other of which is considered "false." In some languages, the integer value zero is considered false and the integer value one is considered true. Older versions of Python also followed that convention (and this still works arithmetically); in recent versions of Python, there are two special values called `True` and `False` that serve as the values a boolean variable can take. (Note the capitalization matters.) Logical operators that operate on boolean variables are mainly as expected: `and`, `or`, `not`, etc.

True and False are Python's boolean values.

Example 6 (Operations with boolean variables):
Try this in a Python interpreter:

```
a = True
b = False
print a and b
print a or b
print 4 > 5
```

What did you get?

Solution and discussion: The first two lines assign a and b as boolean variables. The first two `print` statements return `False` and `True`, respectively. Remember that `and` requires both operands to be `True` in order to return `True`, while `or` only requires one of the operands be `True` to return `True`. Note that comparison operators (i.e., 4 > 5) yield booleans, so the final `print` line returns `False`.

3.4 NoneType

This is a data type you probably have not seen before. A variable of NoneType can have only a single value, the value `None`. (Yes, the word "None," capitalized as shown, is defined as an actual value in Python, just like `True` and `False`.)

The None value.

Example 7 (Operations with NoneType):
Try this in a Python interpreter:

```
a = None
print a is None
print a == 4
```

What did you get?

Solution and discussion: The first `print` statement will return `True` while the second `print` statement will return `False`.
The `is` operator compares "equality" not in the sense of value (like `==` does) but in the sense of memory location. You can type in "a == None",

Logical equality and is.

the better syntax for comparing to None is "a is None".[2] The a == 4 test is false because the number 4 is not equal to None.

Using None to safely initialize a parameter. So what is the use of a variable of NoneType? I use it to "safely" initialize a parameter. That is to say, I initialize a variable to None, and if later on my program tries to do an operation with the variable before the variable has been reassigned to a non-NoneType variable, Python will give an error. This is a simple way to make sure I did not forget to set the variable to a real value. Remember variables are dynamically typed, so replacing a NoneType variable with some other value later on is no problem!

3.5 Lists and tuples

Lists are mutable ordered sequences. Lists are ordered sequences. They are like arrays (in Fortran, IDL, etc.), except each of the items in the list do not have to be of the same type. A given list element can also be set to anything, even another list. Square brackets ("[]") **delimit** (i.e., start and stop) a list, and commas between list elements separate elements from one another. If you have a one element list, put a comma after the element.

List element indices start with 0. List element addresses start with zero, so the first element of list a is a[0], the second is a[1], etc. IDL follows this convention but Fortran does not. Because the ordinal value (i.e., first, second, third, etc.) of an element differs from the address of an element (i.e., zero, one, two, etc.), when we refer to an element by its address we will append a "th" to the end of the address. That is, the "zeroth" element by address is the first element by position in the list, the "oneth" element by address is the second element by position, the "twoth" element by address is the third element by position, and so on.

The len function returns the length of lists and tuples. Finally, the length of a list can be obtained using the len function, e.g., len(a) to find the length of the list a.

Example 8 (A list):

Type in the following in the Python interpreter:

```
a = [2, 3.2, 'hello', [-1.2, 'there', 5.5]]
```

---
[2] The reason is a little esoteric; see the web page http://jaredgrubb.blogspot.com/2009/04/python-is-none-vs-none.html if you're interested in the details (accessed August 16, 2012).

3.5. LISTS AND TUPLES

What is `len(a)`? What does `a[1]` equal to? How about `a[3]`? `a[3][1]`?

Solution and discussion: The `len(a)` is 4, `a[1]` equals 3.2, `a[3]` equals the list `[-1.2, 'there', 5.5]`, and `a[3][1]` equals the string `'there'`. I find the easiest way to read a complex reference like `a[3][1]` is from left to right, that is, "in the threeth element of the list a, take the oneth element."

Referencing list elements that are lists.

In Python, list elements can also be addressed starting from the end; thus, `a[-1]` is the last element in list a, `a[-2]` is the next to last element, etc.

You can create new lists that are slices of an existing list. Slicing follows these rules:

Indexing from the end of a sequence.

- Element addresses in a range are separated by a colon.

- The lower limit of the range is *inclusive,* and the upper limit of the range is *exclusive.*

Slicing rules.

Example 9 (Slicing a list):

Consider again the list a that you just typed in for Example 8. What would `a[1:3]` return?

Solution and discussion: You should get the following if you print out the list slice `a[1:3]`:

```
>>> print a[1:3]
[3.2, 'hello']
```

Because the upper-limit is exclusive in the slice, the threeth element (i.e., the fourth element) is not part of the slice; only the oneth and twoth (i.e., second and third) elements are part of the slice.

Lists are **mutable** (i.e., you can add and remove items, change the size of the list). One way of changing elements in a list is by assignment (just like you would change an element in a Fortran, IDL, etc. array):

Example 10 (Changing list element values by assignment):

Let's go back to the list in Example 8:

3.5. LISTS AND TUPLES

```
a = [2, 3.2, 'hello', [-1.2, 'there', 5.5]]
```

How would we go about replacing the value of the second element with the string 'goodbye'?

Solution and discussion: We refer to the second element as a[1], so using variable assignment, we change that element by:

```
a[1] = 'goodbye'
```

The list a is now:

```
[2, 'goodbye', 'hello', [-1.2, 'there', 5.5]]
```

Python lists, however, also have special "built-in" functions that allow you to insert items into the list, pop off items from the list, etc. We'll discuss the nature of those functions (which are called **methods**; this relates to object-oriented programming) in detail in Ch. 7. Even without that discussion, however, it is still fruitful to consider a few examples of using list methods to alter lists:

Example 11 (Changing lists using list methods):
Assume we have the list we defined in Example 8:

```
a = [2, 3.2, 'hello', [-1.2, 'there', 5.5]]
```

What do the following commands give you when typed into the Python interpreter?:

- a.insert(2,'everyone')
- a.remove(2)
- a.append(4.5)

The insert, remove, and append methods for lists.

Solution and discussion: The first command insert inserts the string 'everyone' into the list after the twoth (i.e., third) element of the list. The second command remove removes the first occurrence of the value given in the argument. The final command append adds the argument to the end of the list.

For the list a, if we printed out the contents of a after each of the above three lines were executed one after the other, we would get:

```
[2, 3.2, 'everyone', 'hello', [-1.2, 'there', 5.5]]
[3.2, 'everyone', 'hello', [-1.2, 'there', 5.5]]
[3.2, 'everyone', 'hello', [-1.2, 'there', 5.5], 4.5]
```

Tuples are nearly identical to lists with the exception that tuples cannot be changed (i.e., they are **immutable**). That is to say, if you try to insert an element in a tuple, Python will return an error. Tuples are defined exactly as lists except you use parenthesis as delimiters instead of square brackets, e.g., b = (3.2, 'hello').

Tuples are immutable ordered sequences.

Note: You can, to an extent, treat strings as lists. Thus, if a = "hello", then a[1:3] will return the substring "el".

Slicing strings as if each character were a list element.

3.6 Exercises with lists and tuples

Remember that exercises are no less necessary than examples to attempt! The only real difference between exercises and examples is that the former are more complex than the latter; pedagogically speaking, both types of problems are used in a similar way, and in my discussion of both examples and exercises, I will often introduce new topics.

▷ **Exercise 4 (Making and changing a list):**

1. Take your street address and make it a list variable myaddress where each token is an element. Make numbers numbers and words strings.

2. What would be the code to set the sum of the numerical portions of your address list to a variable called address_sum?

3. What would be the code to change one of the string elements of the list to another string (e.g., if your address had "West" in it, how would you change that string to "North")?

Solution and discussion: We give the solutions for each of the questions above:

1. For my work address, the myaddress list is:

```
myaddress = [3225, 'West', 'Foster', 'Avenue',
             'Chicago', 'IL', 60625]
```

Line continuation in Python.

Note that when you type in a list in Python, you can break the list after the completion of an element and continue the list on the next line, and Python will automatically know the list is being continued (leading blank spaces are ignored). In general, however, you continue a line of code in Python by putting a backslash ("\") at the end of a line, with nothing after the backslash. Thus, you can also enter the above list by typing in:

```
myaddress = [3225, 'West', 'Foster', 'Avenue', \
             'Chicago', 'IL', 60625]
```

2. This sets the sum of the numerical portions to `address_sum`:

$$\text{address\_sum} = \text{myaddress[0]} + \text{myaddress[-1]}$$

3. Code to change "West" to "North":

$$\text{myaddress[1]} = \text{"North"}$$

▷ **Exercise 5 (Altering the order of a list's elements):**
Take the list you created in Exercise 4 and change the street portion of `myaddress` to have the street first and the building number at the end. Hints: Make use of assignments and slicing.

Solution and discussion: To change the street portion of `myaddress` and view the result:

```
a = myaddress[0]
b = myaddress[1:3]
myaddress[0:2] = b
myaddress[2] = a
print myaddress
```

Assigning sublists. Note that you can assign sublists of a list in one fell swoop if the value on the right can be parsed element-wise (e.g., is also a list of the same length).

3.7 Dictionaries

Definition of a dictionary. Like lists and tuples, dictionaries are also collections of elements, but dictionaries, instead of being ordered, are *unordered* lists whose elements are referenced by *keys*, not by position. Keys can be anything that can be uniquely named and sorted. In practice, keys are usually integers or strings. Values can be anything. (And when I say "anything," I mean *anything*, just like lists and tuples. We'll see in Ch. 6 a little of the broad range of values that dictionaries can hold and how that is a useful feature.) Dictionaries are very powerful; this one data structure revolutionized my code.

Curly braces ("{}") delimit a dictionary. The elements of a dictionary are "key:value" pairs, separated by a colon. Dictionary elements are referenced like lists, except the key is given in place of the element address. The example below will make this all clearer:

Example 12 (A dictionary):
Type the following in the Python interpreter:

```
a = {'a':2, 'b':3.2, 'c':[-1.2, 'there', 5.5]}
```

For the dictionary a:

- What does a['b'] return?

- What does a['c'][1] return?

Solution and discussion: a['b'] returns the floating point number 3.2. a['c'] returns the list [-1.2, 'there', 5.5], so a['c'][1] returns the oneth element of that list, the string 'there'.

Like lists, dictionaries come with "built-in" functions (methods) that enable you to find out all the keys in the dictionary, find out all the values in the dictionary, etc. In Ch. 7, when we introduce OOP, we'll discuss the nature of methods in detail, but even without that discussion, it is still useful to consider a few examples of dictionary methods:

Example 13 (A few dictionary methods):
Assume we have the dictionary from Example 12 already defined in the Python interpreter:

```
a = {'a':2, 'b':3.2, 'c':[-1.2, 'there', 5.5]}
```

If you typed the following into the Python interpreter, what would you get for each line?:

3.8. EXERCISES WITH DICTIONARIES

- d = a.keys()

- d = a.values()

- a.has_key('c')

The keys, values, and has_key methods.

Solution and discussion: The first line executes the command **keys**, which returns a list of all the keys of **a**, and sets that list to the variable **d**. The second command does this same thing as the first command, except d is a list of the values in the dictionary a. The third command tests if dictionary a has an element with the key 'c', returning **True** if true and **False** if not. For the dictionary a, the first line returns the list ['a', 'c', 'b'] and sets that to the variable d while the second line returns **True**.

Do not assume dictionaries are stored in any particular order.

Note that the **keys** and **values** methods do *not* return a sorted list of items. Because dictionaries are *unordered* collections, you *must not* assume the key:value pairs are stored in the dictionary in any particular order. If you want to access the dictionary values in a specific order, you should first order the dictionary's keys (or, in some cases, values) in the desired order using a sorting function like **sorted**. (Section 7.9.1 gives an example of the use of **sorted**.)

3.8 Exercises with dictionaries

▷ **Exercise 6 (Create a dictionary):**

Create a dictionary **myaddress** using your address. Choose relevant keys (they will probably be strings), and separate your address into street address, city, state, and postal code portions, all of which are strings (for your ZIP Code, don't enter it in as a number).

Solution and discussion: For my work address:

```
myaddress = {'street':'3225 West Foster Avenue',
             'city':'Chicago', 'state':'IL',
             'zip':'60625'}
```

As with lists and tuples, I don't need to specify the line continuation character if I break the line in-between the specifications for each element.

▷ **Exercise 7 (Using elements from a dictionary):**
Create a variable `full_address` that is the concatenation of all the elements of the `myaddress` variable from Exercise 6; in your concatenation, include commas and blank spaces as needed. Hint: Remember that commas and blanks can be made into strings.

Solution and discussion: Here's my solution for my `myaddress` from Exercise 6:

```
full_address = myaddress['street'] + ', ' \
             + myaddress['city'] + ', ' \
             + myaddress['state'] + ' ' \
             + myaddress['zip']
```

Notice how when I choose keys that have a clear meaning, in this case labels like "street" and "city," my references to the values in the dictionary associated with those keys read sensibly: `myaddress['street']` makes more sense than `myaddress[0]`. This is one benefit of dictionaries over lists and tuples.

Dictionaries allow you to choose meaningful keys.

3.9 Functions

Functions in Python, in theory, work *both* like functions and subroutines in Fortran, in that (1) input comes via arguments and (2) output occurs through: a return variable (like Fortran functions) and/or arguments (like Fortran subroutines). In practice, functions in Python are written to act like Fortran functions, with a single output returned. (The return value is specified by the `return` statement.) If you want multiple returns, it's easier to put them into a list or use objects.

Functions work like Fortran functions and subroutines.

Function definitions begin with a `def` statement, followed by the name of the function and the argument list in parenthesis. The contents of the function after this `def` line are indented in "*x*" spaces (where "*x*" is a constant). Usually, people indent 4 spaces. (In practice, if you use a development environment like IDLE, or the Python mode in vi or Emacs, you don't have to add the indentation yourself; the environment does it for you.) Example 14 below shows how the indentation works to indicate what lines are inside the function.

All lines in a statement block are usually indented in 4 spaces.

3.9. FUNCTIONS

Important side note: All block structures in Python use indentation to show when they begin and end. This convention is in lieu of "end" lines like `end do` and `end if` in Fortran. For those of us who have had experience using the fixed-form format of Fortran 77, this will seem like a bad idea. For now, just trust me that this indentation convention actually makes your code clearer, more readable, and more concise.

Example 14 (A function):
Type the following in a file (remember to use four spaces for the indentation instead of a tab or another number of spaces):

```
def area(radius):
    area = 3.14 * (radius**2)
    return area
```

What happens if you run the file? Why did nothing happen? Now type the following in the interpreter or Python Shell:

```
a = area(3)
print a
```

What happens?

Functions are defined by def and used by calling.

Solution and discussion: In the first case, nothing happened because you only defined the function; the function was not called. In the second case, you call the function, set the return value to the variable a, and print out a to the screen. Note that in such a simple function, you could have skipped creating the local variable `area` and just typed:

```
    return 3.14 * (radius**2)
```

which would have evaluated the expression prior to the return.

Note how the indentation shows that the two lines of code after the `def` line are the lines inside the function (i.e., they are the code that does the function's tasks).

Positional and keyword arguments.

As we said earlier, inputs to a function, in general, come in via the argument list while the output is the return value of the function. Python accepts both positional and keyword arguments in the argument list of a function: Positional arguments are usually for *required* input while keyword arguments

3.9. FUNCTIONS

are usually for *optional* input. Typically, keyword arguments are set to some default value. If you do not want to have a default value set for the keyword, a safe practice is to just set the keyword to None.

Example 15 (A function with both positional and keyword arguments):
Type the following in a file:

```
def area(radius, pi=None):
    area = pi * (radius**2)
    return area
a = area(3)
```

What happens if you run the file?

Solution and discussion: You should have received an error like this (note I handwrapped the last line to make it fit on the page):

```
Traceback (most recent call last):
  File "example.py", line 4, in <module>
    a = area(3)
  File "example.py", line 2, in area
    area = pi * (radius**2)
TypeError: unsupported operand
          type(s) for *: 'NoneType' and 'int'
```

Because in your a = area(3) call you did not define the keyword argument pi, when the function was called, it used the default value of None for pi. When the function tried to execute an arithmetic operation using pi, an error was raised and execution was transferred to the main program level, where execution finally stopped.

If you type in the following in the interpreter or Python Shell, after first executing the code in *yourfilename.py* (where *yourfilename.py* is the name of the file in which you defined the area function):[3]

```
a = area(3, pi=3.14)
print a
```

---

[3] Recall you execute a file either by typing in python -i yourfilename.py at the command-line or by running the module in IDLE.

3.9. FUNCTIONS

you will get a print-to-screen of the answer, 28.26. Upon the call of **area**, the value of 3.14 was set to **pi** in the function.

Traditionally, Fortran and similar procedural language programmers have had to deal with the problem of lengthy and unwieldy argument lists: If you want to pass in 30 variables, your argument list has 30 variables in it. (It is not surprising to see such subroutine calls in a climate model.) A list of such a length is an undetected error waiting to happen; one typing slip and you could be passing in surface roughness instead of humidity!

A simpler, compact way of passing in lists of arguments.
Python has a nifty way of passing in lists of positional and keyword arguments in one fell swoop by considering a list of positional arguments as a list/tuple and a collection of keyword arguments as a dictionary. You can then use all of Python's built-in list and dictionary methods to manage your function's arguments, with the function's **calling** line only having two variables. This example illustrates how to do this:

Example 16 (Passing in lists of positional and keyword arguments):
Try typing in the following in the same file where you defined the version of **area** with both positional and keyword arguments (i.e., the version in Example 15):

```
args = [3,]
kwds = {'pi':3.14}
a = area(*args, **kwds)
print a
```

then run your file from the Unix command line by:

```
python -i yourfilename.py
```

(or using the shell in IDLE). Remember to put these lines *after* your definition of **area**; otherwise, you will not have an **area** function to refer to ☺.

Solution and discussion: This code should work exactly the same as Example 15, that is:

```
a = area(*args, **kwds)
```

works the same as:

```
a = area(3, pi=3.14)
```

where `args` and `kwds` are given as above. You will get a print-to-screen of the answer, 28.26.

Example 16 illustrates the following rules for passing in function arguments by lists and dictionaries:

- In the function call, put an asterisk (*) before the list that contains the positional arguments and put two asterisks before the dictionary that contains the keyword arguments.

- The list of positional arguments is a list where each element in the list is a positional argument to be passed in, and the list is ordered in the same order as the positional arguments.

- The dictionary of keyword arguments uses string keys corresponding to the name of the keyword and the value of the key:value pairs as the value set to the keyword parameter.

3.10 Logical constructs

The syntax for if-statements is

    `if <condition>:`

if statements.

followed by the block of code to execute if *<condition>* is true. Because indentation delimits the contents of the `if` block, there is no need for an "endif" line.

Example 17 (A compound `if` statement):
Type the following in a file:

```
a = 3
if a == 3:
    print 'I am a ', a
elif a == 2:
    print 'I am a 2'
else:
    print 'I am not a 3 or 2'
```

The compound `elif` statement.

First guess what you think will happen if you run the file (what do you think `elif` does? `else`?) then run the file. What did you get? What would you need to change to get `I am a 2` or `I am not a 3 or 2` to be output to the screen?

Solution and discussion: Because `a = 3`, the first `if` test will test true and `I am a  3` will be printed to the screen.

The `elif` statement is used after the first test and means "else if", or "if the previous `if` was not true, consider this `if`". You can have any number of `elif`s after the initial `if` and the compound `if` statement will go through each one, testing the line's condition and executing what is in the block under the `elif` line if true (then exiting the compound `if`) and going on to the next test if false.

The `else` executes if none of the other `if` and `elif` statements tested true and is ignored otherwise.

> **Remember the colon after `if`, etc.!** Don't forget the colon at the end of `if`, `elif`, and `else` statements! It's easy to forget them ☺ (same with the `def` statement for defining functions).

3.11 Looping

3.11.1 Looping a definite number of times

The standard loop in Python begins with `for` and has the syntax:

  `for <index> in <list>:`

> **The `for` loop goes through a sequence of items.** followed by the contents of the loop. (Don't forget the colon at the end of the `for` line.) The `for` loop is kind of different compared to the Fortran `do` loops you might be familiar with. In Fortran, IDL, etc. you specify a beginning value and an ending value (often 1 and an integer n) for an index, and the loop runs through all integers from that beginning value to that ending value, setting the index to that value. In Python, the loop index runs through a list of items, and the index is assigned to each item in that list, one after the other, until the list of items is exhausted.

Example 18 (A `for` loop):

Type the following in a file (remember to indent 4 spaces in the second line):

```
for i in [2, -3.3, 'hello', 1, -12]:
    print i
```

Run the file. What did you get?

Solution and discussion: The code prints out the elements of the list to screen, one element per line:

```
2
-3.3
hello
1
-12
```

This means `i` changes type as the loop executes. It starts as an integer, becomes floating point, then becomes a string, returns to being an integer, and ends as an integer.

Recall that elements in a Python list can be of *any* type, and that list elements do not all have to be of the same type. Also remember that Python is dynamically typed, so that a variable will change its type to reflect whatever it is assigned to at any given time. Thus, in a loop, the loop index could, potentially, be changing in type as the loop runs through all the elements in a list, which was the case in Example 18 above. Since the loop index does not have to be an integer, it doesn't really make sense to call it an "index;" in Python, it's called an iterator. Note too that since the iterator is not just a number, but an object, you have access to all of the **attributes** and methods of its class (again, more on this in Ch. 7). *Iterators are different than Fortran looping indices.*

A lot of the time you will loop through lists. Technically, however, Python loops can loop through any data structure that is **iterable,** i.e., a structure where after you've looked at one element of it, it will move you onto the next element. Arrays (which we'll cover in Ch. 4) are another iterable structure. *You can loop through any iterable.*

In Fortran, we often loop through arrays by the addresses of the elements. So too in Python, often, you will want to loop through a list by list element addresses. To make this easier to do there is a built-in function called `range` which produces such a list: `range(n)` returns the list $[0, 1, 2, \ldots, n-1]$. *The `range` function makes a list of indices.*

Example 19 (A `for` loop using the `range` function):
Type the following in a file:

3.11. LOOPING

```
a = [2, -3, 'hello', 1, -12]
for i in range(5):
    print a[i]
```

Run the file. What did you get?

Solution and discussion: This code will give the exact same results as in Example 18. The function call `range(5)` produces the list:

```
[0, 1, 2, 3, 4]
```

which the iterator `i` runs through, and which is used as the index for elements in list `a`. Thus, `i` is an integer for every step of the loop.

3.11.2 Looping an indefinite number of times

The while loop. Python also has a `while` loop. It's like any other while loop and begins with the syntax:

>while *<condition>*:

The code block (indented) that follows the `while` line is executed while *<condition>* evaluates as `True`. Here's a simple example:

Example 20 (A `while` loop):
Type in the following into a file (or the interpreter):

```
a = 1
while a < 10:
    print a
    a = a + 1
```

What did you get?

Solution and discussion: This will print out the integers one through ten, with each integer on its own line. Prior to executing the code block underneath the `while` statement, the interpreter checks whether the condition (a < 10) is true or false. If the condition evaluates as `True`, the code block executes; if the condition evaluates as `False`, the code block is not executed. Thus:

```
a = 10
while a < 10:
    print a
    a = a + 1
```

will do nothing. Likewise:

```
a = 10
while False:
    print a
    a = a + 1
```

will also do nothing. In this last code snippet, the value of the variable `a` is immaterial; as the condition is always set to `False`, the `while` loop will never execute. (Conversely, a `while True:` statement will never terminate. It is a bad idea to write such a statement ☺.)

Please see your favorite Python reference if you'd like more information about `while` loops (my reference suggestions are given in Ch. 10). Because they are not as common as their `for` cousins (at least in AOS applications), I won't spend exercise time on them.

3.12 Exercises on functions, logical constructs, and looping

▷ **Exercise 8 (Looping through a list of street address elements):**

Take the list of the parts of your street address from Exercise 4. Write a loop that goes through that list and prints out each item in that list.

Solution and discussion: My street address list was:

```
myaddress = [3225, 'West', 'Foster', 'Avenue', \
             'Chicago', 'IL', 60625]
```

The following loop will do the job:

```
for i in myaddress:
    print i
```

3.12. EXERCISES ON FUNCTIONS, LOGICAL CONSTRUCTS, AND LOOPING

as will this loop:

```
for i in range(len(myaddress)):
    print myaddress[i]
```

Remember the built-in `len` function returns the length of the list that is its argument; the length is an integer and is the argument passed into the `range` call. Note also that the type of `i` behaves differently in the two loops. Python is dynamically typed!

▷ **Exercise 9 (Looping through a list of temperatures and applying a test):**

Pretend you have the following list of temperatures T:

T = [273.4, 265.5, 277.7, 285.5]

and a list of flags called `Tflags` that is initialized to all `False`. `Tflags` and T are each the same size. Thus:

Tflags = [False, False, False, False]

Write a loop that checks each temperature in T and sets the corresponding `Tflags` element to `True` if the temperature is above the freezing point of water.

Solution and discussion: The following loop will do the job:

```
for i in range(len(T)):
    if T[i] > 273.15:
        Tflags[i] = True
```

Remember I'm assuming both T and `Tflags` are already defined before I enter the loop.

▷ **Exercise 10 (A function to loop through a list of temperatures and apply a test):**

Turn your answer to Exercise 9 into a function. Assume that T is the input argument and `Tflags` is what you will want to return from the function. A hint: You can create a four-element list whose values all equal `False` by typing [False]*4. Thus:

Tflags = [False]*4

does the same thing as:

```
Tflags = [False, False, False, False]
```

Also, you may want to use the `range` and `len` functions at some point in your code.

Solution and discussion: The following function will do the job:

```
def temptest(T):
    Tflags = [False]*len(T)
    for i in range(len(T)):
        if T[i] > 273.15:
            Tflags[i] = True
    return Tflags
```

3.13 Modules

Python calls libraries "**modules**" and "**packages**," where a package is a collection of modules. (Usually, people say "module" to refer to both modules and packages, since they're used very similarly. I'll do that for most of this book.) Unlike compiled languages like Fortran, however, these modules are not collections of object files but rather regular Python source code files. A module is a single source code file and a package is a directory containing source code files (and possibly subdirectories of source code files).

Modules and packages.

To **import** a module, Python provides a command called `import`, and its syntax is:

Importing a module.

```
import <module name>
```

Let's look at an example to help our discussion of how to import and use Python modules:

Example 21 (Importing a module):

To import a module called NumPy (this is Python's array package, which we'll talk about in-depth in Ch. 4), type:

```
import numpy
```

Type this in the Python interpreter. It should execute without any message being printed to the screen.

3.13. MODULES

Referring to functions, etc. in a module. Once a module is imported, you can use functions, variables, etc. defined in the module by referring to the imported name (here **numpy**), putting a period ("."), and the name of the function, variable, etc. that was defined in the module. Thus, to use the **sin** function in the package, refer to **numpy.sin**.

Try typing:

```
a = numpy.sin(4)
```

This will return the sine of 4 and set it to the variable **a**. Print out **a** to check this worked correctly; it should equal −0.756, approximately (I truncated most of the digits that the **print** statement provides).

Importing and namespaces. What **import** essentially does is to run the code file that has the filename of *<module name>.py*. When **import** runs that code file, it runs the file in its own little "interpreter." This "interpreter," however, is not a separate Python session but occurs in the current session within a variable named after the module's name. That is to say, the **import** executes the module's code in its own **namespace;** that namespace is a variable with the same name as the module's name.

For **import numpy**, the filename that would be run is *numpy.py* and the contents of that file would be run in the namespace **numpy**. (This isn't quite what happens for NumPy, because NumPy is technically a package of many files, not a module of a single file, but the principle is the same.) If all the module file does is define functions, variables, etc., then nothing will be output. But you have access to everything that is defined by typing the module name, a period, then the name of the module function, variable, etc. you want (hence, **numpy.sin**, etc.). Just as in a regular Python session you have access to all the variables, functions, etc. you define in that regular session, with an imported module, all the variables, functions, etc. that the module created and used are also sitting inside the module's namespace, ready for you to access, using the syntax just mentioned.

Referring to submodules. Submodules (which are subdirectories inside the package directory) are also specified with the periods. For instance, NumPy has a submodule called **ma**, which in turn has special functions defined in it. The submodule then is referred to as **numpy.ma** and the **array** function in the submodule as **numpy.ma.array**.

(As an aside, sometimes the name of a module as written or spoken is different from name that goes in the **import** command: NumPy is the module name, but the namespace is **numpy**, the Scientific Python package has a namespace Scientific, and so on. This is confusing, but unfortunately some modules are this way.)

The idea of a namespace for Python modules helps protect against collisions. In Fortran, you have to be careful you do not duplicate function and subroutine names when you compile against multiple libraries, because if there is a function of the same name in two libraries, one of those will be overwritten. With Python modules, this kind of collision cannot occur, because functions are attached to modules by name through the imported module's namespace. It is, however, possible to defeat this feature and cause collisions if you really want to (e.g., by having duplicate module names in *PYTHONPATH* directories or improper use of from ... import), which is why I am teaching you the safe way of importing rather than the risky way ☺.

How namespaces prevent collisions.

Sometimes, if you use a module a lot, you will want refer to it by a shorter name. To do this, use the import *<module>* as *<alias>* construct, for instance:

```
import numpy as N
```

Then, N.sin is the same as numpy.sin.

Finally, remember, modules can contain data in addition to functions. The syntax to refer to those module data variables is exactly the same as for functions. Thus, numpy.pi gives the value of the mathematical constant π.

Modules can contain data variables in addition to functions.

3.14 A brief introduction to object syntax

While we introduced some elements of objects with Section 3.5 on lists and tuples and Section 3.7 on dictionaries, and while we're saving a rigorous introduction to objects for Ch. 7), at this time, having talked about the syntax for modules, we should briefly introduce a little of what objects are and how in Python to refer to objects and their parts.

The key idea of objects is that variables shouldn't be thought of as having only values (and type), but rather they should be thought of entities that can have any number of other things "attached" to them. If the attached thing is a piece of data, it's called an attribute of the object variable. If the attached thing is a function, it's called a method.

From a syntax viewpoint, if you have an object variable that has many things attached to it, the question is how to refer to those attached things. In Python, the key syntax idea is borrowed from module syntax: Just as you describe functions attached to modules by giving the module name, a period,

Referring to object attributes and methods.

3.15. EXERCISE THAT INCLUDES USING A MODULE

then the function name, you describe things attached to a Python object by giving the variable name, a period, then the attribute or method name.

The syntax of operations with or by attributes and methods should also seem familiar to you: If you want to call an object's methods, you use the same syntax as for functions (i.e., with a calling list given by parenthesis); attributes of objects are in turn read and set attributes just like they were regular variables (i.e., with an equal sign).

Thus, for instance, if I have a list object `mylist`, and I want to use one of the methods attached to that object (e.g., `reverse`), I would type in `mylist.reverse()`. This method reverses all the elements in the object, in place, and so it does not require the passing in of any arguments: The data to reverse is in `mylist` itself (note the empty argument list between the parenthesis).

Using `dir` to see what is attached to an object. If you can attach attributes and methods to an object, you will want a way of viewing all the attributes and methods that are attached. A good interactive development environment will give nicely formatted ways to do this, but if all you have is a Python interpreter, type `dir(x)`, where `x` is the object name, to list (approximately) all attributes and methods attached to an object.

Lastly, as a teaser, here's an idea I want you to think about prior to our introduction of objects in Ch. 7: Nearly everything in Python is an object. Everything. Thus, what I've been calling variables (integers, floats, strings, lists, etc.) are not variables in the traditional Fortran, IDL, Matlab, etc. sense but instead objects. Even functions are objects. This feature of Python will end up having profound implications and will enable us to write programs we never could in other languages traditionally used in the atmospheric and oceanic sciences.

3.15 Exercise that includes using a module

▷ **Exercise 11 (Using functions from a module to do calculations on data):**

Pretend you have the list of temperatures T you saw earlier:

```
T = [273.4, 265.5, 277.7, 285.5]
```

Write code that will calculate the average of the maximum and minimum of T. Hint: The NumPy package has a `max` function and a `min` function that can look through a list of numerical values and return the maximum and minimum value, respectively. The single argument they take is the list of numerical values.

Solution and discussion: Here's code that will do the trick:

```
import numpy
T = [273.4, 265.5, 277.7, 285.5]
maxT = numpy.max(T)
minT = numpy.min(T)
avg_max_min = 0.5 * (maxT + minT)
```

3.16 Exception handling

In traditional Fortran, one common way of checking for and processing program error states is to write an "if" test for the error state and then execute a `stop` statement to stop program execution and output an informative message. In Python, you can accomplish the same thing with the `raise` statement: If you want the program to stop when you have an error, you throw an **exception** with a `raise` statement. Here's an example:

Throwing exceptions and raise.

Example 22 (Using `raise`):

Consider the function `area` we defined in Example 15. How would we put in a test to ensure the user would not pass in a negative radius? One answer: We could put in an `if` test for a negative radius and if true, execute a `raise` statement:

```
def area(radius, pi=None):
    if radius < 0:
        raise ValueError, 'radius negative'
    area = pi * (radius**2)
    return area
```

The syntax for `raise` is the command `raise` followed by an exception class (in this case I used the built-in exception class `ValueError`, which is commonly used to denote errors that have to do with bad variable values), then a comma and a string that will be output by the interpreter when the `raise` is thrown.

3.16. EXCEPTION HANDLING

Exceptions are not the same as Fortran stop statements.

Raising an exception is not exactly the same as a Fortran `stop` statement (though sometimes it will act the same). In the latter, program execution stops and you are returned to the operating system level. In the former, an exception stops execution and sends the interpreter up one level to see if there is some code that will properly handle the error. This means that in using `raise`, you have the opportunity to gracefully handle expected errors without causing the entire program to stop executing.

In Example 22, we saw how to create an exception, but I didn't show you how to handle the exception. That is, I didn't show you how in Python to tell the interpreter what to do if a routine it calls throws an exception. The `try/except` statement is Python's exception handler. You execute the block under the `try`, then execute the `except`s if an exception is raised. Consider this example:

Example 23 (Handling an exception):

Assume we have the function `area` as defined in Example 22 (i.e., with the test for a negative radius). Here is an example of calling the function `area` using `try/except` that will gracefully recognize a negative radius and call `area` again with the absolute value of the radius instead as input:

```
rad = -2.5
try:
    a = area(rad, pi=3.14)
except ValueError:
    a = area(abs(rad), pi=3.14)
```

How the interpreter processes a try/except block.

When the interpreter enters the `try` block, it executes all the statements in the block one by one. If one of the statements returns an exception (as the first `area` call will because `rad` is negative), the interpreter looks for an `except` statement at the calling level (one level up from the first `area` call, which is the level of calling) that recognizes the exception class (in this case `ValueError`). If the interpreter finds such an `except` statement, the interpreter executes the block under that `except`. In this example, that block repeats the `area` call but with the absolute value of `rad` instead of `rad` itself. If the interpreter does not find such an `except` statement, it looks another level up for a statement that will handle the exception; this occurs all the way up to the main level, and if no handler is found there, execution of the entire program stops.

In the examples in this section, I used the exception class `ValueError`. There are a number of built-in exception classes which you can find listed in a good Python reference (e.g., `TypeError`, `ZeroDivisionError`, etc.) and which you can use to handle the specific type of error you are protecting against.[4] I should note, however, the better and more advanced approach is to define your own exception classes to customize handling, but this topic is beyond the scope of this book.

Exception classes.

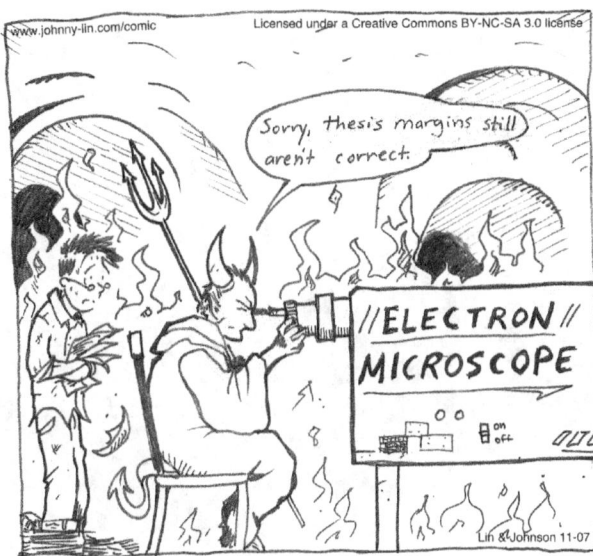

Ph.D. Student Hell

3.17 Summary

In many ways, basic Python variable syntax and control structures look a lot like those in traditional compiled languages. However, Python includes a number of additional built-in data types, like dictionaries, which suggest there will be more to the language than meets the eye; in the rest of this book, we'll find those data structures are *very* powerful (just building up the suspense level ☺). Other features of Python that usually differ from traditional compiled languages include: Python variables are dynamically typed, so they can change type as the program executes; indentation whitespace is significant; imported module names organize the namespace of functions and

---

[4]See http://docs.python.org/library/exceptions.html for a listing of built-in exception classes (accessed August 17, 2012).

3.17. SUMMARY

module data variables; and exceptions can be handled using the `try/except` statement.

The Python style guide.   Finally, seeing all this Python code may make you wonder whether there is a standard style guide to writing Python. Indeed, there is; it's called PEP 8 (PEP stands for "Python Enhancement Proposal") and is online at http://www.python.org/dev/peps/pep-0008.

Chapter 4

Array Operations

4.1 What is an array and the NumPy package

In Ch. 3, we were introduced to lists, which look a lot like Fortran arrays, except lists can hold values of any type. The computational overhead to support that flexibility, however, is non-trivial, and so lists are not practical to use for most scientific computing problems: lists are too slow. To solve this problem, Python has a package called NumPy[1] which defines an array data type that in many ways is like the array data type in Fortran, IDL, etc.

NumPy arrays are like lists except all elements are the same type.

An array is like a list except: All elements are of the same type, so operations with arrays are much faster; multi-dimensional arrays are more clearly supported; and array operations are supported. To utilize NumPy's functions and attributes, you import the package `numpy`. Because NumPy functions are often used in scientific computing, you usually import NumPy as an alias, e.g., `import numpy as N`, to save yourself some typing (see p. 41 for more about importing as an alias). Note that in this chapter and the rest of the book, if you see the alias `N` in code without `import numpy as N` explicitly state, you can assume that `N` was defined by such an import statement somewhere earlier in the code.

Importing NumPy.

4.2 Creating arrays

The most basic way of creating an array is to take an existing list and convert it into an array using the `array` function in NumPy. Here is a basic example:

---

[1] There are other array packages for Python, but the community has now converged on NumPy.

4.2. CREATING ARRAYS

Example 24 (Using the `array` function on a list):
Assume you have the following list:

$$\text{mylist = N.array([[2, 3, -5],[21, -2, 1]])}$$

then you can create an array `a` with:

```
import numpy as N
a = N.array(mylist)
```

Creating arrays using array. The `array` function will match the array type to the contents of the list. Note that the elements of `mylist` have to be convertible to the same type. Thus, if the list elements are all numbers (floating point or integer), the `array` function will work fine. Otherwise, things could get dicey.

Making arrays of a given type. Sometimes you will want to make sure your NumPy array elements are of a specific type. To force a certain numerical type for the array, set the `dtype` keyword to a type code:

Example 25 (Using the `dtype` keyword):
Assume you have a list `mylist` already defined. To make an array `a` from that list that is double-precision floating point, you'd type:

```
import numpy as N
a = N.array(mylist, dtype='d')
```

The dtype keyword and common array typecodes. where the string `'d'` is the **typecode** for double-precision floating point. Some common typecodes (which are all strings) include:

- `'d'`: Double precision floating
- `'f'`: Single precision floating
- `'i'`: Short integer
- `'l'`: Long integer

Often you will want to create an array of a given size and **shape,** but you will not know in advance what the element values will be. To create an

4.2. CREATING ARRAYS

array of a given shape filled with zeros, use the `zeros` function, which takes the shape of the array (a tuple) as the single positional input argument (with `dtype` being optional, if you want to specify it):

Example 26 (Using the `zeros` function):

Let's make an array of zeros of shape (3,2), i.e., three rows and two columns in shape. Type in:

```
import numpy as N
a = N.zeros((3,2), dtype='d')
```

Using `zeros` to create a zero-filled array of a given shape.

Print out the array you made by typing in `print a`. Did you get what you expected?

Solution and discussion: You should have gotten:

```
>>> print a
[[ 0.  0.]
 [ 0.  0.]
 [ 0.  0.]]
```

Note that you don't have to type `import numpy as N` prior to every use of a function from NumPy, as long as earlier in your source code file you have done that import. In the examples in this chapter, I will periodically include this line to remind you that `N` is now an alias for the imported NumPy module. However, in your own code file, if you already have the `import numpy as N` statement near the beginning of your file, you do not have to type it in again as per the example. Likewise, if I do not tell you to type in the `import numpy as N` statement, and I ask you to use a NumPy function, I'm assuming you already have that statement earlier in your code file.

You only have to import NumPy once in your module file.

Also note that while the input shape into `zeros` is a tuple, which all array shapes are, if you type in a list, the function call will still work.

Another array you will commonly create is the array that corresponds to the output of `range`, that is, an array that starts at 0 and increments upwards by 1. NumPy provides the `arange` function for this purpose. The syntax is

The `arange` function.

the same as `range`, but it optionally accepts the `dtype` keyword parameter if you want to select a specific type for your array elements:

Example 27 (Using the `arange` function):

Let's make an array of 10 elements, starting from 0, going to 9, and incrementing by 1. Type in:

    a = N.arange(10)

Print out the array you made by typing in `print a`. Did you get what you expected?

Solution and discussion: You should have gotten:

```
>>> print a
[0 1 2 3 4 5 6 7 8 9]
```

<small>Be careful that `arange` gives you the array *type* you want.</small> Note that because the argument of `arange` is an integer, the resulting array has integer elements. If, instead, you had typed in `arange(10.0)`, the elements in the resulting array would have been floating point. You can accomplish the same effect by using the `dtype` keyword input parameter, of course, but I mention this because sometimes it can be a gotcha: you intend an integer array but accidentally pass in a floating point value for the number of elements in the array, or vice versa.

4.3 Array indexing

<small>Array indices start with 0.</small> Like lists, element addresses start with zero, so the first element of a 1-D array a is `a[0]`, the second is `a[1]`, etc. Like lists, you can also reference elements starting from the end, e.g., element `a[-1]` is the last element in a 1-D array a.

<small>Array slicing rules.</small> Array slicing follows rules very similar to list slicing:

- Element addresses in a range are separated by a colon.

- The lower limit is inclusive, and the upper limit is exclusive.

- If one of the limits is left out, the range is extended to the end of the range (e.g., if the lower limit is left out, the range extends to the very beginning of the array).

- Thus, to specify all elements, use a colon by itself.

Here's an example:

Example 28 (Array indexing and slicing):
Type the following in a Python interpreter:

```
a = N.array([2, 3.2, 5.5, -6.4, -2.2, 2.4])
```

What does a[1] equal? a[1:4]? a[2:]? Try to answer these first without using the interpreter. Confirm your answer by using `print`.

Solution and discussion: You should have gotten:

```
>>> print a[1]
3.2
>>> print a[1:4]
[ 3.2  5.5 -6.4]
>>> print a[2:]
[ 5.5 -6.4 -2.2  2.4]
```

For multi-dimensional arrays, indexing between different dimensions is separated by commas. Note that the fastest varying dimension is always the last index, the next fastest varying dimension is the next to last index, and so forth (this follows C convention).[2] Thus, a 2-D array is indexed [row, col]. Slicing rules also work as applied for each dimension (e.g., a colon selects all elements in that dimension). Here's an example:

Multi-dimensional array indexing and slicing.

Example 29 (Multidimensional array indexing and slicing):
Consider the following typed into a Python interpreter:

```
import numpy as N
a = N.array([[2, 3.2, 5.5, -6.4, -2.2, 2.4],
             [1,  22,   4,  0.1,  5.3,   -9],
             [3,   1, 2.1,   21,  1.1,   -2]])
```

---

[2] See http://docs.scipy.org/doc/numpy/reference/arrays.ndarray.html and the definition of "row-major" in http://docs.scipy.org/doc/numpy/glossary.html (both accessed August 9, 2012).

4.4. EXERCISES IN CREATING AND INDEXING ARRAYS

What is a[1,2] equal to? a[:,3]? a[1,:]? a[1,1:4]?

Solution and discussion: You should have obtained:

```
>>> print a[1,2]
4.0
>>> print a[:,3]
[ -6.4   0.1   21. ]
>>> print a[1,:]
[  1.    22.    4.    0.1    5.3   -9. ]
>>> print a[1,1:4]
[ 22.    4.    0.1]
```

Note that when I typed in the array I did not use the line continuation character at the end of each line because I was entering in a list, and by starting another line after I typed in a comma, Python automatically understood that I had not finished entering the list and continued reading the line for me.

4.4 Exercises in creating and indexing arrays

▷ **Exercise 12 (Creating an array of zeros):**
What is the code to create a 4 row, 5 column array of single-precision floating point zeros and assign it to the variable a?

Solution and discussion: The `zeros` function does the trick. Note that the first argument in the solution is a tuple that gives the shape of the output array, so the first argument needs the extra set of parentheses that says the sequence is a tuple:

```
a = N.zeros((4,5), dtype='f')
```

▷ **Exercise 13 (Using a multidimensional array):**
Consider the example array from Example 29, here repeated:

```
import numpy as N
a = N.array([[2, 3.2, 5.5, -6.4, -2.2, 2.4],
             [1,  22,   4,   0.1,  5.3, -9],
             [3,   1,   2.1, 21,   1.1, -2]])
```

1. What is a[:,3]?

2. What is a[1:4,0:2]? (Why are there no errors from this specification?)

3. What will b = a[1:,2] do? What will b be? Reason out first what will happen, then try it to see. If you were wrong, why were you wrong?

Solution and discussion: My answers:

1. a[:,3] is [-6.4, 0.1, 21].

2. a[1:4,0:2]? selects the last two rows and first three columns as a subarray. There are no errors because while there is no "threeth" row, the row slicing works until it's out of rows.

3. b is the subarray consisting of the last two rows and the third column. The code assigns that subarray to the variable b.

4.5 Array inquiry

Some information about arrays comes through functions that act on arrays; other information comes through attributes attached to the array object. (Remember that basically everything in Python is an object, including arrays. In Section 7.4 we'll be talking more about array attributes.) Let's look at some array inquiry examples:

Example 30 (Array inquiry):
    Import NumPy as the alias N and create a 2-D array a. Below are some array inquiry tasks and the Python code to conduct these tasks. Try these commands out in your interpreter and see if you get what you expect.

Finding the shape, rank, size, and type of an array.

- Return the shape of the array: `N.shape(a)`

- Return the **rank** of the array: `N.rank(a)`

- Return the number of elements in the array: `N.size(a)`

- Typecode of the array: `a.dtype.char`

4.6. ARRAY MANIPULATION

Solution and discussion: Here are some results using the example array from Example 29:

```
>>> print N.shape(a)
(3, 6)
>>> print N.rank(a)
2
>>> print N.size(a)
18
>>> print a.dtype.char
d
```

Note that you should *not* use `len` for returning the number of elements in an array. Also, the `size` function returns the total number of elements in an array. Finally, `a.dtype.char` is an example of an array attribute; notice there are no parentheses at the end of the specification because an attribute variable is a piece of data, not a function that you call.

Use `size`, not `len`, for arrays.

Array inquiry enables you to write flexible code. The neat thing about array inquiry functions (and attributes) is that you can write code to operate on an array in general instead of a specific array of given size, shape, etc. This allows you to write code that can be used on arrays of all types, with the exact array determined at run time.

4.6 Array manipulation

In addition to finding things about an array, NumPy includes many functions to manipulate arrays. Some, like `transpose`, come from linear algebra, but NumPy also includes a variety of array manipulation functions that enable you to massage arrays into the form you need to do the calculations you want. Here are a few examples:

Example 31 (Array manipulation):
Import NumPy as the alias N and create one 6-element 1-D array a, one 8-element 1-D array b, and one 2-D array c (of any size and shape). Below are some array manipulation tasks and the Python code to conduct those tasks. Try these commands out in your interpreter and see if you get what you expect.

Reshaping, transposing, and other array manipulation functions.

- Reshape the array and return the result, e.g.:

```
N.reshape(a,(2,3))
```

- Transpose the array and return the result:

  ```
  N.transpose(c)
  ```

  (Note that I'm asking you to use `transpose` on the 2-D array; the transpose of a 1-D array is just the 1-D array.)

- Flatten the array into a 1-D array and return the result:

  ```
  N.ravel(a)
  ```

- Concatenate arrays and return the result:

  ```
  N.concatenate((a,b))
  ```

  Note that the function `concatenate` has *one* positional argument (not two, as the above may seem to suggest). That one argument is a tuple of the arrays to be concatenated. This is why the above code has "double" parenthesis.

- Repeat array elements and return the result, e.g.:

  ```
  N.repeat(a,3)
  ```

- Convert array a to another type, e.g.:

  ```
  d = a.astype('f')
  ```

  Converting an array to another type.

  The argument of `astype` is the typecode for `d`. This is an example of an object method; we'll explain array object methods more in Section 7.4.

Solution and discussion: Here's my solution for arrays `a` and `b`, where `a = N.arange(6)` and `b = N.arange(8)`, and the 2-D array from Example 29 is now set to the variable `c`:

4.6. ARRAY MANIPULATION

```
>>> print N.reshape(a,(2,3))
[[0 1 2]
 [3 4 5]]
>>> print N.transpose(c)
[[  2.    1.    3. ]
 [  3.2  22.    1. ]
 [  5.5   4.    2.1]
 [ -6.4   0.1  21. ]
 [ -2.2   5.3   1.1]
 [  2.4  -9.   -2. ]]
>>> print N.ravel(a)
[0 1 2 3 4 5]
>>> print N.concatenate((a,b))
[0 1 2 3 4 5 0 1 2 3 4 5 6 7]
>>> print N.repeat(a,3)
[0 0 0 1 1 1 2 2 2 3 3 3 4 4 4 5 5 5]
>>> d = a.astype('f')
>>> print d
[ 0.  1.  2.  3.  4.  5.]
```

You'll want to consult a NumPy reference (see Section 10.3) to get a full list of the array manipulation functions available, but here's one more snazzy function I wanted to mention. In the atmospheric and oceanic sciences, we often find ourselves using 2-D regularly gridded slices of data where the *x*- and *y*-locations of each array element is given by the corresponding elements of the *x* and *y* vectors. Wouldn't it be nice to get a 2-D array whose elements are the *x*-values for each column and a 2-D array whose elements are the *y*-values for each row? The `meshgrid` function does just that:

The `meshgrid` function.

Example 32 (The `meshgrid` function):
Consider the following code that creates two vectors, `lon` and `lat`, that hold longitude and latitude values (in degrees), respectively, and then assigns the result of `N.meshgrid(lon,lat)` to a variable a:

```
import numpy as N
lon = N.array([0, 45, 90, 135, 180, 225, 270, 315, 360])
lat = N.array([-90, -45, 0, 45, 90])
a = N.meshgrid(lon,lat)
```

What type is a? What is a[0]? a[1]?

Solution and discussion: The variable a is a tuple of two elements. The first element of a, i.e., a[0], is a 2-D array:

```
>>> print a[0]
[[  0  45  90 135 180 225 270 315 360]
 [  0  45  90 135 180 225 270 315 360]
 [  0  45  90 135 180 225 270 315 360]
 [  0  45  90 135 180 225 270 315 360]
 [  0  45  90 135 180 225 270 315 360]]
```

and the second element of the tuple a, i.e., a[1] is also a 2-D array:

```
>>> print a[1]
[[-90 -90 -90 -90 -90 -90 -90 -90 -90]
 [-45 -45 -45 -45 -45 -45 -45 -45 -45]
 [  0   0   0   0   0   0   0   0   0]
 [ 45  45  45  45  45  45  45  45  45]
 [ 90  90  90  90  90  90  90  90  90]]
```

The columns of a[0] are the longitude values at each location of the 2-D grid whose longitude locations are defined by lon and whose latitude locations are defined by lat. The rows of a[1] are the latitude values at each location of the same 2-D grid (i.e., that grid whose longitude locations are defined by lon and whose latitude locations are defined by lat). Which is what we wanted ☺.

An aside: Note that the first row (i.e., the zeroth row) in a[1] is the first one printed, so going from top-to-bottom, you are moving in latitude values from south-to-north. Thus:

```
>>> print a[1][0,:]
[-90 -90 -90 -90 -90 -90 -90 -90 -90]
```

will print the −90 degrees latitude row in a[1]. Remember that 2-D arrays in NumPy are indexed [row, col], so the slicing syntax [0,:] will select all columns in the first row of a 2-D NumPy array.

4.7 General array operations

So far we've learned how to make arrays, ask arrays to tell us about themselves, and manipulate arrays. But what scientists really want to do with arrays is make calculations with them. In this section, we discuss two ways to do exactly that. Method 1 uses `for` loops, in analogue to the use of loops in traditional Fortran programming, to do element-wise array calculations. Method 2 uses array syntax, where looping over array elements happens implicitly (this syntax is also found in Fortran 90 and later versions, IDL, etc.).

4.7.1 General array operations: Method 1 (loops)

Using for loops to operate on arrays.

The tried-and-true method of doing arithmetic operations on arrays is to use loops to examine each array element one-by-one, do the operation, and then save the result in a results array. Here's an example:

Example 33 (Multiply two arrays, element-by-element, using loops):
Consider this code:

```
import numpy as N
a = N.array([[2, 3.2, 5.5, -6.4],
             [3,   1, 2.1,   21]])
b = N.array([[4, 1.2,  -4,  9.1],
             [6,  21, 1.5,  -27]])
shape_a = N.shape(a)
product_ab = N.zeros(shape_a, dtype='f')
for i in xrange(shape_a[0]):
    for j in xrange(shape_a[1]):
        product_ab[i,j] = a[i,j] * b[i,j]
```

Can you describe what is happening in each line? (We haven't talked about `xrange` yet, but take a guess as to what it does.)

Solution and discussion: In the first four lines after the `import` line (lines 2–5), I create arrays `a` and `b`. They are both two row, four column arrays. In the sixth line, I read the shape of array `a` and save it as the variable `shape_a`. Note that `shape_a` is the tuple (2,4). In the seventh line, I create a results array of the same shape of `a` and `b`, of single-precision floating point type, and with each element filled with zeros. In the last three lines (lines 8–10), I loop through all rows (the number of which is given by `shape_a[0]`) and all columns (the number of which is given by `shape_a[1]`), by index.

4.7. GENERAL ARRAY OPERATIONS

Thus, `i` and `j` are set to the element addresses for rows and columns, respectively, and line 10 does the multiplication operation and sets the product in the results array `product_ab` using the element addresses.

So, what is the `xrange` function? Recall that the `range` function provides an *n*-element list of the integers 0 to *n* − 1, incremented by 1, and is useful for providing the element addresses for lists (and arrays). The `range` function creates the entire list in memory when it is called, but for the purposes of looping through list/array element addresses, we're not interested in being able to access all the addresses all the time; we only need the element address for the current loop iteration. That's what `xrange` does; it provides only one element of the array element addresses list at a time. This makes the loop more efficient.

The `xrange` function makes looping more efficient.

One other note: In this example, I make the assumption that the shape of `a` and the shape of `b` are the same, but I should instead add a check that this is actually the case. While a check using an `if` statement condition such as:

Do not use logical equality to check equality between sequences.

   N.shape(a) != N.shape(b)

will work, because equality between sequences is true if all corresponding elements are equal,[3] things get tricky, fast, if you are interested in more complex logical comparisons and boolean operations for arrays. For instance, the logic that works for != doesn't apply to built-in Python boolean operators such as `and`. We'll see later on in Section 4.8.2 how to do element-wise boolean operations on arrays.

So, why wouldn't you want to use the looping method for general array operations? In three and a half words: Loops are (relatively) s-l-o-w. Thus, if you can at all help it, it's better to use array syntax for general array operations: your code will be faster, more flexible, and easier to read and test.

Loops are slower than array syntax.

4.7.2 General array operations: Method 2 (array syntax)

The basic idea behind array syntax is that, much of the time, arrays interact with each other on a corresponding element basis, and so instead of requiring the user to write out the nested `for` loops explicitly, the loops and element-wise operations are done implicitly in the operator. That is to say, instead of writing this code (assume arrays `a` and `b` are 1-D arrays of the same size):

What is array syntax?

---

[3]See the "Built-in Types" entry in the online Python documentation at http://docs.python.org/library/stdtypes.html#sequence-types-str-unicode-list-tuple-bytearray-buffer-xrange (accessed March 26, 2012).

4.7. GENERAL ARRAY OPERATIONS

```
c = N.zeros(N.shape(a), dtype='f')
for i in xrange(N.size(a)):
    c[i] = a[i] * b[i]
```

array syntax means you can write this code:

```
c = a * b
```

Let's try this with a specific example using actual numbers:

Example 34 (Multiply two arrays, element-by-element, using array syntax):

Type the following in a file and run it using the Python interpreter:

```
import numpy as N
a = N.array([[2, 3.2, 5.5, -6.4],
             [3,   1, 2.1,   21]])
b = N.array([[4, 1.2,  -4, 9.1],
             [6,  21, 1.5, -27]])
product_ab = a * b
```

What do you get when you print out `product_ab`?

Solution and discussion: You should get something like this:

```
>>> print product_ab
[[  8.     3.84  -22.    -58.24]
 [ 18.    21.     3.15 -567.  ]]
```

Arithmetic operators act element-wise by default on NumPy arrays. In this example, we see that arithmetic operators are automatically defined to act element-wise when operands are NumPy arrays or scalars. (Operators do have function equivalents in NumPy, e.g., `product`, `add`, etc., for the situations where you want to do the operation using function syntax.) Additionally, the output array c is automatically created on assignment; there is no need to initialize the output array using `zeros`.

Array syntax already checks compatibility. There are three more key benefits of array syntax. First, operand shapes are automatically checked for compatibility, so there is no need to check for that explicitly. Second, you do not need to know the rank (i.e., whether it is 1-D, 2-D, etc.) of the arrays ahead of time, so the same line of code works

4.7. GENERAL ARRAY OPERATIONS

on arrays of *any* rank. Finally, the array syntax formulation runs faster than the equivalent code using loops! Simpler, better, faster: pretty cool, eh? ☺

Let's try another array syntax example:

Example 35 (Another array syntax example):

Type the following in a Python interpreter:

```
import numpy as N
a = N.arange(10)
b = a * 2
c = a + b
d = c * 2.0
```

What results? Predict what you think a, b, and c will be, then print out those arrays to confirm whether you were right.

Solution and discussion: You should get something like this:

```
>>> print a
[0 1 2 3 4 5 6 7 8 9]
>>> print b
[ 0  2  4  6  8 10 12 14 16 18]
>>> print c
[ 0  3  6  9 12 15 18 21 24 27]
>>> print d
[  0.   6.  12.  18.  24.  30.  36.  42.  48.  54.]
```

Arrays a, b, and c are all integer arrays because the operands that created those arrays are all integers. Array d, however, is floating point because it was created by multiplying an integer array by a floating point scalar. Python automatically chooses the type of the new array to retain, as much as possible, the information found in the operands.

4.7. GENERAL ARRAY OPERATIONS

4.7.3 Exercise on general array operations

▷ **Exercise 14 (Calculate potential temperature from arrays of T and p):**
Write a function that takes a 2-D array of pressures (p, in hPa) and a 2-D array of temperatures (T, in K) and returns the corresponding potential temperature, assuming a reference pressure (p_0) of 1000 hPa. Thus, the function's return value is an array of the same shape and type as the input arrays. Recall that potential temperature θ is given by:

$$\theta = T \left(\frac{p_0}{p}\right)^\kappa$$

where κ is the ratio of the gas constant of dry air to the specific heat of dry air at constant pressure and equals approximately 0.286.

Solution and discussion: I will give two different solutions: one using loops and the other using array syntax. Using loops, you get:

```
import numpy as N
def theta(p, T, p0=1000.0, kappa=0.286):
    shape_input = N.shape(p)
    output = N.zeros(shape_input, dtype='f')
    for i in xrange(shape_input[0]):
        for j in xrange(shape_input[1]):
            output[i,j] = T[i,j] * (p0 / p[i,j])**(kappa)
    return output
```

Remember to use `return` when passing a result out of a function.

Note the use of keyword input parameters to provide potentially adjustable constants. Remember, to return anything from a function, you have to use the `return` command.

Using array syntax, the solution is even terser:

```
import numpy as N
def theta(p, T, p0=1000.0, kappa=0.286):
    return T * (p0 / p)**(kappa)
```

and the array syntax solution works for arrays of any rank, not just 2-D arrays.

An aside on documenting code: Python has a robust set of standardized ways to generate code documentation. The most basic construct, as you might guess, is the humble but ever-important comment line. The pound sign ("#") is Python's comment character, and all text after that symbol is ignored by the interpreter.

Python's comment character.

The most basic, specialized, built-in construct for documenting code is the **docstring.** These are strings set in triple quotes that come right after a `def` statement in a function. Here is my array syntax solution to Exercise 14 with a docstring added:

Documenting with the docstring.

```
import numpy as N
def theta(p, T, p0=1000.0, kappa=0.286):
    """Calculate the potential temperature.

    Returns a NumPy array of potential temperature that is
    the same size and shape as the input parameters.  The
    reference pressure is given by p0 and kappa is the
    ratio of the gas constant for dry air to the specific
    heat of dry air at constant pressure.

    Input parameters:
        :p:  Pressure [hPa].  NumPy array of any rank.
        :T:  Temperature [K].  NumPy array of any rank.
    """
    return T * (p0 / p)**(kappa)
```

Finally, there are a number of document generation packages that automatically convert Python code and code docstrings into web documentation. In the docstring example I give above, I use some reStructuredText conventions that will be nicely typeset by the Sphinx documentation generator. See http://docutils.sf.net/rst.html and http://sphinx.pocoo.org for details.

The Sphinx documentation generation package.

4.8 Testing inside an array

Often times, you will want to do calculations on an array that involves conditionals. For instance, you might want to loop through an array of data and check if any values are negative; if any exist, you may wish to set those elements to zero. To accomplish the first part of that task, you need to do some kind of testing while going through an array.

In Python, there are a few ways of doing this. The first is to implement this in a loop. A second way is to use array syntax and take advantage of comparison operators and specialized NumPy search functions.

4.8.1 Testing inside an array: Method 1 (loops)

In this method, you apply a standard conditional (e.g., `if` statement) while inside the nested `for` loops running through the array. This is similar to

4.8. TESTING INSIDE AN ARRAY

traditional Fortran syntax. Here's is an example:

Example 36 (Using looping to test inside an array):
Say you have a 2-D array `a` and you want to return an array `answer` which is double the value of the corresponding element in `a` when the element is greater than 5 and less than 10, and zero when the value of that element in `a` is not. What's the code for this task?

Solution and discussion: Here's the code:

```
answer = N.zeros(N.shape(a), dtype='f')
for i in xrange(N.shape(a)[0]):
    for j in xrange(N.shape(a)[1]):
        if (a[i,j] > 5) and (a[i,j] < 10):
            answer[i,j] = a[i,j] * 2.0
        else:
            pass
```

The pass command in blocks that do nothing. The `pass` command is used when you have a block statement (e.g., a block `if` statement, etc.) where you want the interpreter to do nothing. In this case, because `answer` is filled with all zeros on initialization, if the `if` test condition returns `False`, we want that element of `answer` to be zero. But, all elements of `answer` start out as zero, so the `else` block has nothing to do; thus, we `pass`.

Again, while this code works, loops are slow, and the `if` statement makes it even slower. The nested `for` loops also mean that this code will only work for a 2-D version of the array `a`.

4.8.2 Testing inside an array: Method 2 (array syntax)

Is there a way we can do testing inside an array while using array syntax? That way, we can get the benefits of simpler code, the flexibility of code that works on arrays of any rank, and speed. The answer is, yes! Because NumPy has comparison and boolean operators that act element-wise and array inquiry and selection functions, we can write a variety of ways of testing and selecting inside an array while using array syntax. Before we discuss some of those ways, we need some context about using NumPy comparison operators and boolean array functions.

4.8. TESTING INSIDE AN ARRAY

NumPy comparison operators and boolean array functions

NumPy has defined the standard comparison operators in Python (e.g., ==, <) to work element-wise with arrays. Thus, if you run these lines of code:

```
import numpy as N
a = N.arange(6)
print a > 3
```

the following array is printed out to the screen:

```
[False False False False True True]
```

Each element of the array a that was greater than 3 has its corresponding element in the output set to `True` while all other elements are set to `False`. You can achieve the same result by using the corresponding NumPy function `greater`. Thus:

```
print N.greater(a, 3)
```

gives you the same thing. Other comparison functions are similarly defined for the other standard comparison operators; those functions also act element-wise on NumPy arrays.

Using comparison operators on arrays generate boolean arrays.

Once you have arrays of booleans, you can operate on them using boolean operator NumPy functions. You cannot use Python's built-in **and**, **or**, etc. operators; those will not act element-wise. Instead, use the NumPy functions `logical_and`, `logical_or`, etc. Thus, if we have this code:

Must use NumPy functions to do boolean operations on arrays.

```
a = N.arange(6)
print N.logical_and(a>1, a<=3)
```

the following array will be printed to screen:

```
[False False True True False False]
```

The `logical_and` function takes two boolean arrays and does an element-wise boolean "and" operation on them and returns a boolean array of the same size and shape filled with the results.

With this background on comparison operators and boolean functions for NumPy arrays, we can talk about ways of doing testing and selecting in arrays while using array syntax. Here are two methods: using the **where** function and using arithmetic operations on boolean arrays.

4.8. TESTING INSIDE AN ARRAY

The where function

IDL users will find this function familiar. The Python version of **where**, however, can be used in two ways: To directly select corresponding values from another array (or scalar), depending on whether a condition is true, and to return a list of array element indices for which a condition is true (which then can be used to select the corresponding values by selection with indices).

The syntax for using **where** to directly select corresponding values is the following:

Using where to get values when a condition is true.

$$\texttt{N.where}(\textit{<condition>}, \textit{<value if true>}, \textit{<value if false>})$$

If an element of *<condition>* is `True`, the corresponding element of *<value if true>* is used in the array returned by the function, while the corresponding element of *<value if false>* is used if *<condition>* is `False`. The **where** function returns an array of the same size and shape as *<condition>* (which is an array of boolean elements). Here is an example to work through:

Example 37 (Using where to directly select corresponding values from another array or scalar):
Consider the following case:

```
import numpy as N
a = N.arange(8)
condition = N.logical_and(a>3, a<6)
answer = N.where(condition, a*2, 0)
```

What is `condition`? `answer`? What does the code do?

Solution and discussion: You should get:

```
>>> print a
[0 1 2 3 4 5 6 7]
>>> print condition
[False False False False  True  True False False]
>>> print answer
[ 0  0  0  0  8 10  0  0]
```

The array `condition` shows which elements of the array `a` are greater than 3 and less than 6. The **where** call takes every element of array `a` where that is

4.8. TESTING INSIDE AN ARRAY

true and doubles the corresponding value of a; elsewhere, the output element from **where** is set to 0.

The second way of using **where** is to return a tuple of array element indices for which a condition is true, which then can be used to select the corresponding values by selection with indices. (This is like the behavior of IDL's **WHERE** function.) For 1-D arrays, the tuple is a one-element tuple whose value is an array listing the indices where the condition is true. For 2-D arrays, the tuple is a two-element tuple whose first value is an array listing the row index where the condition is true and the second value is an array listing the column index where the condition is true. In terms of syntax, you tell **where** to return indices instead of an array of selected values by calling **where** with only a single argument, the *<condition>* array. To select those elements in an array, pass in the tuple as the argument inside the square brackets (i.e., []) when you are selecting elements. Here is an example:

Using where to get the indices where a condition is true.

Example 38 (Using where to return a list of indices):
Consider the following case:

```
import numpy as N
a = N.arange(8)
condition = N.logical_and(a>3, a<6)
answer_indices = N.where(condition)
answer = (a*2)[answer_indices]
```

What is `condition`? `answer_indices`? `answer`? What does the code do?

Solution and discussion: You should have obtained similar results as Example 37, except the zero elements are absent in **answer** and now you also have a tuple of the indices where **condition** is true:

```
>>> print a
[0 1 2 3 4 5 6 7]
>>> print condition
[False False False False  True  True False False]
>>> print answer_indices
(array([4, 5]),)
>>> print answer
[ 8 10]
```

4.8. TESTING INSIDE AN ARRAY

The array `condition` shows which elements of the array `a` are greater than 3 and less than 6. The `where` call returns the indices where `condition` is true, and since `condition` is 1-D, there is only one element in the tuple `answer_indices`. The last line multiplies array `a` by two (which is also an array) and selects the elements from that array with addresses given by `answer_indices`.

Using where to obtain indices will return a 1-D array.

Note that selection with `answer_indices` will give you a 1-D array, even if `condition` is not 1-D. Let's turn array `a` into a 3-D array, do everything else the same, and see what happens:

```
import numpy as N
a = N.reshape( N.arange(8), (2,2,2) )
condition = N.logical_and(a>3, a<6)
answer_indices = N.where(condition)
answer = (a*2)[answer_indices]
```

The result now is:

```
>>> print a
[[[0 1]
  [2 3]]

 [[4 5]
  [6 7]]]
>>> print condition
[[[False False]
  [False False]]

 [[ True  True]
  [False False]]]
>>> print answer_indices
(array([1, 1]), array([0, 0]), array([0, 1]))
>>> print answer
[ 8 10]
```

Note how `condition` is 3-D and the `answer_indices` tuple now has three elements (for the three dimensions of `condition`), but `answer` is again 1-D.

4.8. TESTING INSIDE AN ARRAY

Arithmetic operations using boolean arrays

You can also accomplish much of what the `where` function does in terms of testing and selecting by taking advantage of the fact that arithmetic operations on boolean arrays treat `True` as 1 and `False` as 0. By using multiplication and addition, the boolean values become selectors, because any value multiplied by 1 or added to 0 is that value. Let's see an example of how these properties can be used for selection:

Example 39 (Using arithmetic operators on boolean arrays as selectors):
Consider the following case:

```
import numpy as N
a = N.arange(8)
condition = N.logical_and(a>3, a<6)
answer = ((a*2)*condition) + \
         (0*N.logical_not(condition))
```

Solution and discussion: The solution is the same as Example 37:

```
>>> print a
[0 1 2 3 4 5 6 7]
>>> print condition
[False False False False  True  True False False]
>>> print answer
[ 0  0  0  0  8 10  0  0]
```

But how does this code produce this solution? Let's go through it step-by-step. The `condition` line is the same as in Example 37, so we won't say more about that. But what about the `answer` line? First, we multiply array `a` by two and then multiply that by `condition`. Every element that is `True` in `condition` will then equal double of `a`, but every element that is `False` in `condition` will equal zero. We then add that to zero times the `logical_not` of `condition`, which is `condition` but with all `True`s as `False`s, and vice versa. Again, any value that multiplies by `True` will be that value and any value that multiplies by `False` will be zero. Because `condition` and its "logical not" are mutually exclusive—if one is true the other is false—the sum of the two terms to create `answer` will select either `a*2` or `0`. (Of course, the array generated by `0*N.logical_not(condition)` is an array of zeros, but you can see how multiplying by something besides `0` will give you a different replacement value.)

Using arithmetic with boolean arrays as conditional selectors.

4.8. TESTING INSIDE AN ARRAY

Also, note the continuation line character is a backslash at the end of the line (as seen in the line that assigns `answer`).

This method of testing inside arrays using arithmetic operations on boolean arrays is also faster than loops.

A simple way of seeing how fast your code runs.
An aside on a simple way to do timings: The time module has a function `time` that returns the current system time relative to the Epoch (a date that is operating system dependent). If you save the current time as a variable before and after you execute your function/code, the difference is the time it took to run your function/code.

Example 40 (Using `time` to do timings):
Type in the following and run it in a Python interpreter:

```
import time
begin_time = time.time()
for i in xrange(1000000L):
    a = 2*3
print time.time() - begin_time
```

What does the number that is printed out represent?

Solution and discussion: The code prints out the amount of time (in seconds) it takes to multiply two times three and assign the product to the variable a one million times. (Of course, it also includes the time to do the looping, which in this simple case probably is a substantial fraction of the total time of execution.)

4.8.3 Exercise on testing inside an array

▷ **Exercise 15 (Calculating wind speed from u and v):**
Write a function that takes two 2-D arrays—an array of horizontal, zonal (east-west) wind components (u, in m/s) and an array of horizontal, meridional (north-south) wind components (v, in m/s)—and returns a 2-D array of the magnitudes of the total wind, if the wind is over a minimum magnitude,

and the minimum magnitude value otherwise. (We might presume that in this particular domain only winds above some minimum constitute "good" data while those below the minimum are indistinguishable from the minimum due to noise or should be considered equal to the minimum in order to properly represent the effects of some quantity like friction.)

Thus, your input will be arrays u and v, as well as the minimum magnitude value. The function's return value is an array of the same shape and type as the input arrays.

Solution and discussion: I provide two solutions, one using loops and one using array syntax. Here's the solution using loops:

```
import numpy as N
def good_magnitudes(u, v, minmag=0.1):
    shape_input = N.shape(u)
    output = N.zeros(shape_input, dtype=u.dtype.char)
    for i in xrange(shape_input[0]):
        for j in xrange(shape_input[1]):
            mag = ((u[i,j]**2) + (v[i,j]**2))**0.5
            if mag > minmag:
                output[i,j] = mag
            else:
                output[i,j] = minmag
    return output
```

Here's the solution using array syntax, which is terser and works with arrays of all ranks:

```
import numpy as N
def good_magnitudes(u, v, minmag=0.1):
    mag = ((u**2) + (v**2))**0.5
    output = N.where(mag > minmag, mag, minmag)
    return output
```

4.9 Additional array functions

NumPy has many array functions, which include basic mathematical functions (`sin`, `exp`, `interp`, etc.) and basic statistical functions (`correlate`, `histogram`, `hamming`, `fft`, etc.). For more complete lists of array functions, see Section 10.3 for places to look. From the Python interpreter, you

See other listings for more array functions.

can also use `help(numpy)` as well as `help(numpy.x)`, where x is the name of a function, to get more information.

4.10 Summary

In this chapter, we saw that NumPy is a powerful array handling package that provides the array handling functionality of IDL, Matlab, Fortran 90, etc. We learned how to use arrays using the traditional Fortran-like method of nested `for` loops, but we also saw how array syntax enables you to write more streamlined and flexible code: The same code can handle operations on arrays of arbitrary rank. With NumPy, Python can be used for all of the traditional data analysis calculation tasks commonly done in the atmospheric and oceanic sciences. Not bad, for something that's free ☺.

Climatology Horror Films

Chapter 5

File Input and Output

The atmospheric and oceanic sciences (AOS) are "data" intensive fields, whether data refers to observations or model output. Most of the analysis we do involve datasets, and so facilities for file input/output (i/o) are critical. Fortunately, Python has very robust facilities for file i/o. In this chapter, we will sort-of touch on those facilities.

Why do I say "sort-of?": because I am in somewhat of a quandary when it comes to talking about file input/output. On the one hand, I want to show you how to use routines that you will want to use for your own research and analysis. On the other hand, because this book is an introduction to Python, I want to show you the fundamentals of how to do things in the language. In Python, the most robust file i/o packages, while not difficult to use, are still rather conceptually advanced.[1] The introduction of these packages might distract from the larger goal of showing you the fundamentals. As a compromise, this chapter will describe ways of handling file i/o that, while not the most efficient or optimized, nonetheless will work for many (if not most) AOS uses and which illustrate basic methods in using Python (this is particularly true when I discuss handling strings). In the summary in Section 5.4, I will briefly describe additional packages for file i/o that you may want to look into.

In this chapter we will look at input/output to and from text files and netCDF files. But before we do so, I want to make some comments about file objects, which are foundational to how Python interfaces with a file, whether text, netCDF, or another format.

---

[1] An example is the PyTables package, a really great package for large datasets that utilizes some very advanced optimization methods.

5.1 File objects

File objects represent the file to the interpreter. A file object is a "variable" that represents the file to Python. This is a subtle but real difference with procedural languages. For instance, in Fortran, you use functions to operate on a file and unit numbers to specify the file you're operating on (e.g., read(3,*), where 3 is the unit number that represents the file to Fortran). In Python, you use methods attached to file objects to operate on the file. (More on objects is in Ch. 7.)

Creating file objects using the open statement. File objects are created like any other object in Python, that is, by assignment. For text files, you **instantiate** a file object with the built-in open statement:

```
fileobj = open('foo.txt', 'r')
```

The first argument in the open statement gives the filename. The second argument sets the mode for the file: 'r' for reading-only from the file, 'w' for writing a file, and 'a' for appending to the file.

Creating netCDF file objects. Python has a number of modules available for handling netCDF files; for the netCDF package we'll be using in this chapter, there is a different command to create file objects that correspond to the netCDF file, but the syntax is similar:

```
fileobj = S.NetCDFFile('air.mon.mean.nc',
                       mode='r')
```

As with open, the string 'r' means read, etc. In Section 5.3, when we discuss netCDF input/output in more detail, I'll explain the rest of the syntax of the above file object creation statement. For now, I just want to point out that the file object fileobj is created by assignment to the return of the S.NetCDFFile command.

The close method of file objects. One method common to both the text and netCDF file objects we'll be looking at is the close method, which, as you might expect, closes the file object. Thus, to close a file object fileobj, execute:

```
fileobj.close()
```

5.2 Text input/output

Once you've created the text file object, you can use various methods attached to the file object to interact with the file.

5.2.1 Text input/output: Reading a file

To read one line from the file, use the `readline` method:

```
aline = fileobj.readline()
```

Because the file object is connected to a text file, `aline` will be a string. Note that `aline` contains the newline character, because each line in a file is terminated by the newline character.

To read the rest of a file that you already started reading, or to read an entire file you haven't started reading, and then put the read contents into a list, use the `readlines` method:

The readlines method.

```
contents = fileobj.readlines()
```

Here, `contents` is a list of strings, and each element in `contents` is a line in the `fileobj` file. Each element also contains the newline character, from the end of each line in the file.

Note that the variable names `aline` and `contents` are not special; use whatever variable name you would like to hold the strings you are reading in from the text file.

5.2.2 Text input/output: Writing a file

To write a string to the file that is defined by the file object `fileobj`, use the `write` method attached to the file object:

```
fileobj.write(astr)
```

Here, `astr` is the string you want to write to the file. Note that a newline character is *not* automatically written to the file after the string is written. If you want a newline character to be added, you have to append it to the string prior to writing (e.g., `astr+'\n'`).

To write a list of strings to the file, use the `writelines` method:

The writelines method; write and writelines do not write newline by default.

```
fileobj.writelines(contents)
```

Here, `contents` is a list of strings, and, again, a newline character is *not* automatically written after the string (so you have to explicitly add it if you want it written to the file).

5.2.3 Text input/output: Processing file contents

Let's say you've read-in the contents of a file from the file and now have the file contents as a list of strings. How do you do things with them? In particular, how do you turn them into numbers (or arrays of numbers) that you can analyze? Python has a host of string manipulation methods, built-in to string variables (a.k.a., objects), which are ideal for dealing with contents from text files. We will mention only a few of these methods.

The string method split.
The `split` method of a string object takes a string and breaks it into a list using a separator. For instance:

```
a = '3.4 2.1 -2.6'
print a.split(' ')
['3.4', '2.1', '-2.6']
```

will take the string `a`, look for a blank space (which is passed in as the argument to `split`, and use that blank space as the delimiter or separator with which one can split up the string.

The string method join.
The `join` method takes a separator string and puts it between items of a list (or an array) of strings. For instance:

```
a = ['hello', 'there', 'everyone']
'\t'.join(a)
'hello\tthere\teveryone'
```

will take the list of strings `a` and concatenate these elements together, using the tab string (`'\t'`) to separate two elements from each other. (For a short list of some special strings, see p. 19.)

Converting strings to numerical types.
Finally, once we have the strings we desire, we can convert them to numerical types in order to make calculations. Here are two ways of doing so:

- If you loop through a list of strings, you can use the `float` and `int` functions on the string to get a number. For instance:

```
import numpy as N
anum = N.zeros(len(a), 'd')
for i in xrange(len(a)):
    anum[i] = float(a[i])
```

5.2. TEXT INPUT/OUTPUT

takes a list of strings `a` and turns it into a NumPy array of double-precision floating point numbers `anum`.[2]

- If you make the list of strings a NumPy array of strings, you can use the `astype` method for type conversion to floating point or integer. For instance:

  ```
  anum = N.array(a).astype('d')
  ```

  takes a list of strings `a`, converts it from a list to an array of strings using the `array` function, and turns that array of strings into an array of double-precision floating point numbers `anum` using the `astype` method of the array of strings.

A gotcha: Different operating systems may set the end-of-line character to something besides '\n'. Make sure you know what your text file uses. (For instance, MS-DOS uses '\r\n', which is a carriage return followed by a line feed.) By the way, Python has a platform independent way of referring to the end-of-line character: the attribute `linesep` in the module os. If you write your program using that variable, instead of hard-coding in '\n', your program will write out the specific end-of-line character for the system you're running on.

Different OSes have different end-of-line characters.

Example 41 (Writing and reading a single column file):
Take the following list of temperatures T:

```
T = [273.4, 265.5, 277.7, 285.5]
```

write it to a file *one-col_temp.txt*, then read the file back in.

Solution and discussion: This code will do the trick (note I use comment lines to help guide the reader):

---

[2] Note that you can specify the array `dtype` without actually writing the `dtype` keyword; NumPy array constructors like `zeros` will understand a typecode given as the second positional input parameter.

5.2. TEXT INPUT/OUTPUT

```
import numpy as N

outputstr = ['\n']*len(T)              #- Convert to string
for i in xrange(len(T)):               #  and add newlines
    outputstr[i] = \
        str(T[i]) + outputstr[i]

fileout = open('one-col_temp.txt', 'w')  #- Write out
fileout.writelines(outputstr)            #  to the
fileout.close()                          #  file

filein = open('one-col_temp.txt', 'r')   #- Read in
inputstr = filein.readlines()            #  from the
filein.close()                           #  file

Tnew = N.zeros(len(inputstr), 'f')       #- Convert
for i in xrange(len(inputstr)):          #  string to
    Tnew[i] = float(inputstr[i])         #  numbers
```

Note you don't have to strip off the newline character before converting the number to floating point using `float`.

A caveat about reading text files: In the beginning of this chapter, I said I would talk about file reading in a way that teaches the fundamentals of Python, not in a way that gives you the most efficient solution to file i/o for AOS applications. This is particularly true for what I've just told you about reading text files. String methods, while powerful, are probably too low-level to bother with every time you want to read a text file; you'd expect someone somewhere has already written a function that automatically processes text formats typically found in AOS data files. Indeed, this is the case: see the `asciiread` function in PyNGL,[3] the `readAscii` function in the Climate Data Analysis Tools (CDAT),[4] and the SciPy Cookbook i/o page[5] for examples.

---

[3] http://www.pyngl.ucar.edu/Functions/Ngl.asciiread.shtml (accessed August 16, 2012).
[4] http://www2-pcmdi.llnl.gov/cdat/tips_and_tricks/file_IO/reading_ASCII.html (accessed August 16, 2012).
[5] http://www.scipy.org/Cookbook/InputOutput (accessed August 16, 2012).

5.2.4 Exercise to read a multi-column text file

▷ **Exercise 16 (Reading in a multi-column text file):**
You will find the file *two-col_rad_sine.txt* in the *datasets* sub-directory of *course_files*. Write code to read the two columns of data in that file into two arrays, one for angle in radians (column 1) and the other for the sine of the angle (column 2). (The *course_files* directory of files is available online at the book's website. See p. viii for details on obtaining the files. Alternately, feel free to use a text data file of your own.)

The two columns of *two-col_rad_sine.txt* are separated by tabs. The file's newline character is just '\n' (though this isn't something you'll need to know to do this exercise). The file has no headers.

Solution and discussion: Here's my solution:

```
import numpy as N
fileobj = open('two-col_rad_sine.txt', 'r')
data_str = fileobj.readlines()
fileobj.close()

radians = N.zeros(len(data_str), 'f')
sines = N.zeros(len(data_str), 'f')
for i in xrange(len(data_str)):
    split_istr = data_str[i].split('\t')
    radians[i] = float(split_istr[0])
    sines[i] = float(split_istr[1])
```

The array `radians` holds the angles (in radians) and the array `sines` holds the sine of those angles. Note that the above code does not need to know ahead of time how many lines are in the file; all the lines will be read in by the `readlines` method call.

5.3 NetCDF input/output

NetCDF is a platform-independent binary file format that facilitates the storage and sharing of data along with its metadata. Versions of the tools needed to read and write the format are available on practically every operating system and in every major language used in the atmospheric and oceanic sciences.

5.3. NETCDF INPUT/OUTPUT

The structure of netCDF files.

Before discussing how to do netCDF i/o in Python, let's briefly review the structure of netCDF. There are four general types of parameters in a netCDF file: global attributes, variables, variable attributes, and dimensions. Global attributes are usually strings that describe the file as a whole, e.g., a title, who created it, what standards it follows, etc.[6] Variables are the entities that hold data. These include both the data-proper (e.g., temperature, meridional wind, etc.), the domain the data is defined on (delineated by the dimensions), and metadata about the data (e.g., units). Variable attributes store the metadata associated with a variable. Dimensions define a domain for the data-proper, but they also have values of their own (e.g., latitude values, longitude values, etc.), and thus you usually create variables for each dimension that are the same name as the dimension.[7]

As an example of a set of variables and dimensions for a netCDF file, consider the case where you have a timeseries of surface temperature for a latitude-longitude grid. For such a dataset, you would define "lat", "lon", and "time" dimensions and corresponding variables for each of those dimensions. The variable "lat" would be 1-D with the number of elements given for the "lat" dimension and likewise for the variables "lon" and "time", respectively. Finally, you would define the variable "Ts" as 3-D, dimensioned "lat", "lon", and "time".

Several Python packages can read netCDF files, including: the Ultrascale Visualization-Climate Data Analysis Tools (UV-CDAT), CDAT, PyNIO, pysclint, PyTables, and ScientificPython. We'll be discussing ScientificPython in this section, not because it's the best package of this bunch but because it was one of the earliest Python netCDF interfaces, and many subsequent packages have emulated its user-interface.

5.3.1 NetCDF input/output: Reading a file

Importing the ScientificPython netCDF submodule.

ScientificPython is another one of those packages whose "human-readable" name is different from its "imported" name. In addition, the netCDF utilities are in a subpackage of ScientificPython. Thus, the import name for the netCDF utilities is long and you will almost always want to assign the imported package to an alias:

```
import Scientific.IO.NetCDF as S
```

---

[6] It is unfortunate that "global attributes" and "variable attributes" are called attributes, since the term attributes has a very specific meaning in object-oriented languages. When I talk about object attributes in close proximity to netCDF attributes, in this section, I'll try to make the object attributes occurrence glossary-linked.

[7] For more on netCDF, see http://www.unidata.ucar.edu/software/netcdf/docs (accessed August 16, 2012).

The command to create a file object, as we mentioned earlier, is very similar to the **open** command used for text files, except that the constructor is in the subpackage NetCDF and is named `NetCDFFile` (the NetCDF subpackage is itself in the IO subpackage of the Scientific package). The filename is the first argument and you specify the mode in which you wish to open the file by the **mode** keyword input parameter (set to `'r'` for read, `'w'` for write, and `'a'` for append; if you forget to write `mode=`, it will still all work fine). Thus, to open the file *file.nc* in read-only mode, type:

```
fileobj = S.NetCDFFile('file.nc', mode='r')
```

With netCDF files, the conceptualization of a file as a file object has a cognitive benefit. If we think of a file object as being the file itself (as Python sees it), we might expect that the netCDF global attributes should be actual attributes of the file object. Indeed, that is the case, and so, in the case of our above example, if the netCDF file has a global attribute named "title", the file object `fileobj` will have an attribute named `title` (referred to as `fileobj.title`, following the standard Python objects syntax) that is set to the value of the global attribute.

NetCDF file objects have an attribute `variables` which is a dictionary. The keys are strings that are the names of the variables, and the values are variable objects (which is a kind of object specially defined for netCDF handling) that contain the variable's value(s) as well as the variable's metadata (the variable's variable attributes). NetCDF file objects also have an attribute `dimensions` which is a dictionary. The keys are strings that are the names of the dimensions, and the values are the lengths of the dimensions. Let's look at an example of reading a variable named `'Ts'` from a netCDF file:

_{The `variables` attribute is a dictionary of variable objects.}

Example 42 (Reading a variable named 'Ts'):
In this example, we'll read in the data associated with the name `'Ts'` (which is probably surface temperature) and one piece of metadata. Note that the "name" of the variable is a string; I'm not assuming that the "name" is the actual variable itself (i.e., a variable Ts). To do the first task, we will access the data in the variable and put it in a NumPy array. This code would do the trick:

_{Get variable object data values with the `getValue` method.}

```
data = fileobj.variables['Ts'].getValue()
```

The variable is found in the `variables` attribute, which is a dictionary, so we use the variable name as the key (`'Ts'`). What is returned from that dictionary is a special kind of object called a variable object. This object has a method called `getValue` which returns the values of the data in the object,

5.3. NETCDF INPUT/OUTPUT

so we call that method (which takes no arguments, so we pass it an empty argument list). Finally, we use assignment to put the values into the NumPy array `data`.

Our second task is to obtain metadata about `'Ts'`, in particular the units. To do so, we'll read the variable attribute `units` (which gives the units of `'Ts'`) that is attached to the `'Ts'` variable object and save it to a scalar Python variable `unit_str`. Here's the code that would do this:

```
units_str = fileobj.variables['Ts'].units
```

Again, `variables` is an attribute of `fileobj` and is a dictionary. Thus, the `'Ts'` key applied to that dictionary will extract the variable object that contains the data and metadata of `'Ts'`. Variable attributes are attributes of the variable object, so to obtain the units you specify the `units` attribute. Remember, `fileobj.variables['Ts']` gives you a variable object. The `units` attribute is a string, which gets set to the variable `units_str`, and we're done.

Let's put all this together and look at a more complex example of reading a netCDF dataset, in this case, the NCEP/NCAR Reanalysis 1:

Example 43 (Reading a netCDF dataset):

The code below reads the monthly mean surface/near-surface air temperature from the NCEP/NCAR Reanalysis 1 netCDF dataset found in the subdirectory *datasets* of the *course_files* directory. The netCDF file is named *air.mon.mean.nc*. Without running it, what do you expect would be output? Try to explain what each line of the code below does before you read the solution:

```
1  import numpy as N
2  import Scientific.IO.NetCDF as S
3  fileobj = S.NetCDFFile('air.mon.mean.nc', mode='r')
4  print fileobj.title
5  print fileobj.dimensions
6  print fileobj.variables
7  data = fileobj.variables['air'].getValue()
8  print N.shape(data)
9  print data[0:10,30,40]
10 print fileobj.variables['air'].long_name
```

Solution and discussion: The following is output to screen by the code above (note though, because the `print` command does not, in general, word-wrap properly, I put in line breaks after each item in the dictionary and every four items in the `data` listing to make them more readable on this page):

```
Monthly mean air temperature NCEP Reanalysis
{'lat': 73, 'lon': 144, 'time': None}
{'lat': <NetCDFVariable object at 0x2194270>,
 'air': <NetCDFVariable object at 0x2194738>,
 'lon': <NetCDFVariable object at 0x21946a8>,
 'time': <NetCDFVariable object at 0x21946f0>}
(755, 73, 144)
[ 24.64419365  28.36103058  29.27451515  28.94766617
  25.15870857  24.2053318   24.1325798   23.70580482
  23.58633614  23.20644951]
Monthly Mean Air Temperature
```

(Note, in the discussion below, the line numbers refer to the code, not the screen output.) The first line after the NumPy import statement imports the `NetCDF` subpackage of `Scientific.IO` and aliases it to S. The next line creates the file object representation of the netCDF file and sets the mode to read-only. The global attribute `title`, which is the title of the entire file, is printed out in line 4.

In lines 5 and 6, the `dimensions` and `variables` attributes are printed out. As those attributes are dictionaries, key:value pairs are printed out. This shows there are three dimensions (latitude, longitude, and time) and four variables (the dimensions plus the air temperature). Note that the dimension of `'time'` is set to `None` because that dimension is this netCDF file's unlimited dimension (the dimension along which one can append new latitude-longitude slices).

In line 7, the NumPy array `data` is created from the value of the variable named `'air'`, and in the next line, the shape of `data` is printed out. (The array is dimensioned [time, latitude, longitude]; remember that the rightmost dimension is the fastest varying dimension.) In line 9, a subarray of `data` is printed out, the data from the first ten time points at a single physical location. The last line prints out the long name of the variable named `'air'`.

(You can type the code in to run it. Alternately, this code can be found in the *code_files* subdirectory of *course_files*, in the file *example-netcdf.py*.)

5.3. NETCDF INPUT/OUTPUT

The National Center for Atmospheric Research Receives a New Cluster

5.3.2 NetCDF input/output: Writing a file

In order to write out a netCDF file, you first have to create a file object that is set for writing, for instance:

```
fileobj = S.NetCDFFile('file.nc', mode='w')
```

Once the file object exists, you use methods of the file object to create the dimensions and variable objects that will be in the file. You have to create the dimensions before the variable objects (since the latter depends on the former), and you have to create the variable objects first before you fill them with values and metadata.

The `createDimension` method creates a dimension. This method both creates the name of the dimension and sets the value (length) of the dimension. The `createVariable` method creates a variable object; note that it only creates the infrastructure for the variable (e.g., the array shape) and does not fill the values of the variable, set variable attributes, etc.

Filling netCDF array and scalar variables. To fill array variables, use the slicing syntax (i.e., the colon) with the variable object in an assignment operation. (This will make more sense once we see it in the example below.) The values of scalar variables are assigned to the variable object through the `assignValue` method of the *variable object* (not of the file object). Finally, variable attributes are set using Python's regular object assignment syntax, as applied to the variable object.

5.3. NETCDF INPUT/OUTPUT

To illustrate the writing process, let's walk through an example (the example's code can be found in *course_files/code_files* in the file *example-netcdf.py*):

Example 44 (Writing a netCDF file):
What does the following code do?:

```
1   fileobj = S.NetCDFFile('new.nc', mode='w')
2   lat = N.arange(10, dtype='f')
3   lon = N.arange(20, dtype='f')
4   data1 = N.reshape(N.sin(N.arange(200, dtype='f')*0.1),
5                              (10,20))
6   data2 = 42.0
7   fileobj.createDimension('lat', len(lat))
8   fileobj.createDimension('lon', len(lon))
9   lat_var = fileobj.createVariable('lat', 'f', ('lat',))
10  lon_var = fileobj.createVariable('lon', 'f', ('lon',))
11  data1_var = fileobj.createVariable('data1', 'f',
12                                      ('lat','lon'))
13  data2_var = fileobj.createVariable('data2', 'f', ())
14  lat_var[:] = lat[:]
15  lon_var[:] = lon[:]
16  data1_var[:,:] = data1[:,:]
17  data1_var.units = 'kg'
18  data2_var.assignValue(data2)
19  fileobj.title = "New netCDF file"
20  fileobj.close()
```

Solution and discussion: The first line creates the file object connected to the netCDF file we'll be writing to. The lines 2–6, we create the data variables we'll be writing: two vectors, one 2-D array, and one scalar. After that, in line 7, we create the latitude and longitude dimensions (named 'lat' and 'lon', respectively) based on the lengths of the two vectors.

Lines 9–13 create variable objects using the createVariable method of the file object. Note how lat_var will be the variable in the file named 'lat' and is a 1-D variable dimensioned by the dimension named 'lat'. That is to say, the 'lat' in the first argument of createVariable refers to the variable's name while 'lat' in the third argument of createVariable (which is part of a 1-element tuple) refers to the dimension created two code lines above. Variable lon_var is structured in a similar way. Finally, note how because data2_var is a scalar, the dimensioning tuple is empty.

5.3. NETCDF INPUT/OUTPUT

Lines 14–16 fill the three non-scalar variables. These arrays are filled using slicing colons to select both the source values and their destination elements. In the case of line 14, as a specific example, such use of the slicing colon is interpreted as meaning "put the values of the array `lat` into the values of the variable object `lat_var`."

Line 17 attaches a units attribute to the variable object `data1_var`, and line 18 assigns a scalar value to `data2_var`. Line 19 assigns the global attribute `title`, and the final line closes the file attached to the file object.

5.3.3 Exercise to read and write a netCDF file

▷ **Exercise 17 (Read and write a netCDF reanalysis dataset):**
Open the netCDF NCEP/NCAR Reanalysis 1 netCDF dataset of monthly mean surface/near-surface air temperature and read in the values of the `time` variable. (The example data is in the *datasets* subdirectory of *course_files* in the file *air.mon.mean.nc*.)

Alter the time values so that the first time value is 0.0 (i.e., subtract out the minimum of the values). Change the units string to just say `'hours'`, i.e., eliminate the datum. (The original units string from the netCDF file gave a datum.)

Write out the new time data and units as a variable in a new netCDF file.

Solution and discussion: The solution is found in *course_files/code_files* in the file *exercise-netcdf.py* and is reproduced below (with some line continuations added to fit it on the page):

```
1  import numpy as N
2  import Scientific.IO.NetCDF as S
3
4  fileobj = S.NetCDFFile('air.mon.mean.nc', mode='r')
5  time_data = fileobj.variables['time'].getValue()
6  time_units = fileobj.variables['time'].units
7  fileobj.close()
8
9  time_data = time_data - N.min(time_data)
10 time_units = 'hours'
11
12 fileobj = S.NetCDFFile('newtime.nc', mode='w')
13 fileobj.createDimension('time', N.size(time_data))
14 time_var = fileobj.createVariable('time',
15                                  'd', ('time',))
16 time_var.units = time_units
17 time_var[:] = time_data[:]
18 fileobj.title = \
19     "New netCDF file for the time dimension"
20 fileobj.close()
```

Note again how array syntax makes the calculation to eliminate the time datum (line 9) a one-liner ☺.

5.4 Summary

In this chapter we saw that Python conceptualizes files as objects, with attributes and methods attached to them (as opposed to merely unit number addresses). To manipulate and access those files, you use the file object's methods. For the contents of text files, we found string methods to be useful, and for netCDF files, there are a variety of methods that give you the numerical data.

While many of the methods we discussed in this chapter can work for much daily work, you probably will find any one of a number of Python packages to be easier to use when it comes to doing file input/output. These include: UV-CDAT, PyNIO, pysclint, PyTables, etc. Some of these packages include text input/output functions that do line splitting and conversion for you. Some of these packages can also handle other formats such as HDF, GRIB, etc. For a list of more file input/output resources, please see Ch. 10.

5.4. SUMMARY

Chapter 6

A "Real" AOS Project: Putting Together a Basic Data Analysis Routine

At this point, we've covered enough of Python for you to do basically any atmospheric or oceanic sciences calculation you would normally use a data analysis language like IDL or Matlab for (excepting visualization, which we'll cover in Ch. 9). So let's put what we've learned to the test and do a "real" AOS data analysis project.

In Section 6.1, I present your mission (should you accept it ☺). In Sections 6.2–6.5, I give four different ways of solving the problem. Why four solutions? I want to use this real-world-like project to demonstrate how the modern features of Python enable you to write much more powerful and robust programs than are possible in traditional compiled and data analysis languages; you can write a Fortran-like program in Python, but if you do, you'll miss features of Python that can help make your life as a scientist much easier. Finally, we finish with some exercises where we use these modern methods to extend our data analysis program.

6.1 The assignment

Let's say you have three data files named *data0001.txt*, *data0002.txt*, and *data0003.txt*. Each data file contains a single column of data of differing lengths (on the order of thousands of points). The data files have no headers. Write a program that:

- Reads in the data from each file into its own NumPy array.

6.2. SOLUTION ONE: FORTRAN-LIKE STRUCTURE

- Calculates the mean, median, and standard deviation of the values in each data file, saving the values to variables for possible later use.

While you can do this assignment without recourse to a real dataset, there are three data files so structured in the *course_files/datasets* directory. The data is random (Gaussian distributed), with the first dataset *data0001.txt* having a mean and standard deviation of 1, the second *data0002.txt* having a mean and standard deviation of 2, etc., so that you can see whether you're getting the right result. Specifically, NumPy will calculate the mean and standard deviation as:

```
data0001.txt:   0.962398498535   1.00287723892
data0002.txt:   2.02296936035    1.99446291623
data0003.txt:   3.08059179687    2.99082810178
```

Hints: The NumPy function for calculating the mean is `mean`, the median is `median`, and the standard deviation is `std`.

Bath Time at the Coriolis Household

6.2 Solution One: Fortran-like structure

In this solution, I've put all the file open, closing, read, and conversion into a function, so you don't have to type **open**, etc., three times. Then, I make use of NumPy's statistical functions to analyze the data and assign the results

6.2. SOLUTION ONE: FORTRAN-LIKE STRUCTURE

to variables. The way it's written, however, looks very Fortran-esque, with variables initialized and/or created explicitly.

```
import numpy as N

def readdata(filename):
    fileobj = open(filename, 'r')
    outputstr = fileobj.readlines()
    fileobj.close()
    outputarray = N.zeros(len(outputstr), dtype='f')
    for i in xrange(len(outputstr)):
        outputarray[i] = float(outputstr[i])
    return outputarray

data1 = readdata('data0001.txt')
data2 = readdata('data0002.txt')
data3 = readdata('data0003.txt')

mean1 = N.mean(data1)
median1 = N.median(data1)
stddev1 = N.std(data1)

mean2 = N.mean(data2)
median2 = N.median(data2)
stddev2 = N.std(data2)

mean3 = N.mean(data3)
median3 = N.median(data3)
stddev3 = N.std(data3)
```

The program above works fine, but we haven't really taken much advantage of anything unique to Python. How might we change that? For instance, in `readdata`, instead of using a loop to go through each element and convert it to floating point, we could use array syntax and the `astype` method of NumPy array objects. The code to replace lines 7–9 would be:

Example of using `astype` for array type conversion.

```
outputarray = N.array(outputstr)
outputarray = outputarray.astype('f')
```

This doesn't really change much, however. The program is still written so that anytime you specify a variable, whether a filename or data variable, or an analysis function, *you type it in*. This is fine if you have only three files, but what if you have a thousand? Very quickly, this kind of programming becomes not-very-fun.

6.3 Solution Two: Store results in arrays

One approach seasoned Fortran programmers will take to making this code better is to put the results (mean, median, and standard deviation) into arrays and have the element's position in the array correspond to *data0001.txt*, etc. Then, you can use a `for` loop to go through each file, read in the data, and make the calculations. This means you don't have to type in the names of every mean, median, etc. variable to do the assignment. And, since we also have Python's powerful string type to create the filenames, this approach is even easier to do in Python than Fortran. The solution, then, is:

```
import numpy as N
num_files = 3
mean = N.zeros(num_files)
median = N.zeros(num_files)
stddev = N.zeros(num_files)

for i in xrange(num_files):
    filename = 'data' + ('000'+str(i+1))[-4:] + '.txt'
    data = readdata(filename)
    mean[i] = N.mean(data)
    median[i] = N.median(data)
    stddev[i] = N.std(data)
```

(I left out the definition of `readdata`, which is the same as in Solution One. This is also true for all the other solutions to come.)

This code is slightly more compact but scales up to any `num_files` number of files. But I'm still bothered by two things. First, what if the filenames aren't numbered? How then do you relate the element position of the `mean`, etc. arrays to the file the calculated quantity is based on? Variable names (e.g., `mean1`) *do* convey information and connect labels to values; by putting my results into generic arrays, I lose that information. Second, why should I predeclare the size of `mean`, etc.? If Python is dynamic, shouldn't I be able to arbitrarily change the size of `mean`, etc. on the fly as the code executes?

6.4 Solution Three: Store results in dictionaries

Before looking at this solution, we first need to ask how might dictionaries be useful for our problem. We previously said variable names connect labels to values, meaning that a string (the variable name) is associated with a value (scalar, array, etc.). In Python, there is a special construct that can associate a string with a value: a dictionary. From that perspective, setting a value to a key that is the variable name (or something similar), as you do in dictionaries, is effectively the same as setting a variable with an equal sign. However, dictionaries allow you to do this *dynamically* (i.e., you don't have to type in "variable equals value") and will accommodate *any* string, not just those numbered numerically.

Variable names connect labels to values.

Dictionaries can dynamically associate strings with values.

Here, then, is a solution that uses dictionaries to hold the statistical results. The keys for the dictionary entries are the filenames:

```
 1  import numpy as N
 2  mean = {}     #- Initialize as empty dictionaries
 3  median = {}
 4  stddev = {}
 5  list_of_files = ['data0001.txt', 'data0002.txt',
 6                   'data0003.txt']
 7
 8  for ifile in list_of_files:
 9      data = readdata(ifile)
10      mean[ifile] = N.mean(data)
11      median[ifile] = N.median(data)
12      stddev[ifile] = N.std(data)
```

So, in this solution, instead of creating the filename each iteration of the loop, I create a list of files and iterate over that. Here, it's hard-coded in, but this suggests if we could access a directory listing of data files, we could generate such a list automatically. I can, in fact, do this with the `glob` function of the glob module:[1]

Using `glob` to get a directory file listing.

```
import glob
list_of_files = glob.glob("data*.txt")
```

You can sort `list_of_files` using list methods or some other sorting function. (See the discussion on p. 111 which briefly introduces the built-in `sorted` function.)

---
[1] See http://docs.python.org/library/glob.html for details on the module (accessed August 16, 2012).

6.5. SOLUTION FOUR: STORE RESULTS AND FUNCTIONS IN DICTIONARIES

Another feature of this solution is that statistical values are now referenced intelligently. That is to say, if you want to access, say, the mean of *data0001.txt*, you type in `mean['data0001.txt']`. Thus, we've fixed the issue we had in Solution Two, where the element address of the variable `mean` had limited meaning if the dataset filenames were unnumbered. Cool!

An aside: Again, you don't need the continuation backslash if you're continuing elements of a list (or similar entities) in the next line. Also, because of Python's namespace protections (see p. 41 for more details), we can have a variable named `mean` in our program that will not conflict with the NumPy function `mean`, because that function is referred to as `N.mean`.

Example of namespace protection in Python.

6.5 Solution Four: Store results and functions in dictionaries

The last solution was pretty good, but here's one more twist: What if I wanted to calculate more than just the mean, median, and standard deviation? What if I wanted to calculate 10 metrics? 30? 100? Can I make my program flexible in that way?

The answer is, yes! And here too, Python dictionaries save the day: The key:value pairs enable you to put *anything* in as the value, even functions and other dictionaries. So, we'll refactor our solution to store the function objects themselves in a dictionary of functions, linked to the string keys `'mean'`, `'median'`, and `'stddev'`. We will also make a `results` dictionary that will hold the dictionaries of the mean, median, and standard deviation results. That is, `results` will be a dictionary of dictionaries. This solution is:

Dictionaries can hold any object, even functions and other dictionaries.

```
1   import numpy as N
2   import glob
3
4   metrics = {'mean':N.mean, 'median':N.median,
5               'stddev':N.std}
6   list_of_files = glob.glob("data*.txt")
7
8   results = {}                       #- Initialize results
9   for imetric in metrics.keys():     #  dictionary for each
10      results[imetric] = {}          #  statistical metric
11
12  for ifile in list_of_files:
13      data = readdata(ifile)
14      for imetric in metrics.keys():
15          results[imetric][ifile] = metrics[imetric](data)
```

This program is now generally written to calculate mean, median, and standard deviation *for as many files as there are* in the working directory that match `"data*.txt"` and can be extended to calculate *as many statistical metrics as desired*. If you want to access some other files, just change the search pattern in `glob`. If you want to add another statistical metric, just add another entry in the `metrics` dictionary. So, you just change two lines: *nothing else in the program needs to change.* This is what I mean when I say that Python enables you to write code that is more concise, flexible, and robust than in traditional languages. By my lights, this isn't just cool, but *way* cool ☺.

6.6 Exercises on using dictionaries and extending your basic data analysis routine

▷ **Exercise 18 (Dynamically filling a dictionary):**
Assume you're given the following list of files:

```
list_of_files = ['data0001.txt', 'data0002.txt',
                 'data0003.txt']
```

- Create a dictionary `filenum` where the keys are the filenames and the value is the file number (i.e., *data0001.txt* has a file number of 1) as an integer.

- Make your code fill the dictionary automatically, assuming that you have a list `list_of_files`.

- Hints: To convert a string to an integer, use the `int` function on the string, and the list and array sub-range slicing syntax also works on strings.

Solution and discussion: Here's my program to fill `filenum`:

```
filenum = {}
list_of_files = ['data0001.txt', 'data0002.txt',
                 'data0003.txt']
for ifile in list_of_files:
    filenum[ifile] = int(ifile[4:8])
```

▷ **Exercise 19 (Extend your data analysis routine to calculate skew and kurtosis):**

For the basic data analysis routine assignment given in this chapter, extend the last solution so that it also calculates the skew and kurtosis of each file's data. (Hint: NumPy has functions `skew` and `kurtosis` that do the calculations.)

Solution and discussion: Here's my extended program:

```
import numpy as N
import glob

metrics = {'mean':N.mean, 'median':N.median,
           'stddev':N.std, 'skew':N.skew,
           'kurtosis':N.kurtosis}
list_of_files = glob.glob("data*.txt")

results = {}                       #- Initialize results
for imetric in metrics.keys():     #  dictionary for each
    results[imetric] = {}          #  statistical metric

for ifile in list_of_files:
    data = readdata(ifile)
    for imetric in metrics.keys():
        results[imetric][ifile] = metrics[imetric](data)
```

That was easy! (Again, I left out the definition of `readdata` from this code, because it's just the same as in Solution One.)

6.7 Summary

In a traditional Fortran data analysis program, filenames, variables, and functions are all static. That is to say, they're specified by typing. Python data structures enable us to write dynamic programs, because variables are dynamically typed. In particular, Python dictionaries enable you to dynamically associate a name with a variable or function (or anything else), which is essentially what variable assignment does. Thus, dictionaries enable you to add, remove, or change a "variable" on the fly. The results are programs that are more concise and flexible. And fewer lines of code means fewer places for bugs to hide. Way cool!

Chapter 7

An Introduction to OOP Using Python: Part I—Basic Principles and Syntax

7.1 What is object-oriented programming

Object-oriented programming (OOP), deservedly or not, has something of a reputation as an obtuse and mysterious way of programming. You may have heard of it, and even heard that it is a powerful way of writing programs, but you probably haven't heard a clear and concise description of how it works to help you write better AOS programs. Unfortunately, I also cannot give you a clear and concise description of how OOP works to help you program.

The problem is not that I cannot describe to you what an object is or give you a definition of OOP, but rather that any description of the mechanics and use of OOP does not really capture how OOP makes your life easier as a scientist programmer. It's like thinking that a description of oil pigments and poplar surfaces will somehow enable you to "get" how the Mona Lisa works. For both OOP and art, you can't describe the forest in terms of the trees.

Really, the only way I know of to convey how OOP enables atmospheric and oceanic scientists to do better science using a computer is to give you many examples of its use. So, in this chapter, I'll do just that. After a brief description of the mechanics of OOP, we'll look at some simple examples and work through some more complex examples, including examples from the atmospheric and oceanic sciences. Through these examples, I hope to describe both how to write object-oriented programs as well as why object-oriented programs work the way they do.

7.1. WHAT IS OBJECT-ORIENTED PROGRAMMING

7.1.1 Procedural vs. object-oriented programming

One good way of describing something new is to compare it with something old. Most atmospheric and oceanic scientists have had experience with procedural programming, so we'll start there. Procedural programs look at the world in terms of two entities, "data" and "functions." In a procedural context, the two entities are separate from each other. A function takes data as input and returns data as output. Additionally, there's nothing customizable about a function with respect to data. As a result, there are no barriers to using a function on various types of data, even inappropriately.

Procedural programs have data and functions as separate entities.

In the real world, however, we don't think of things or objects as having these two features (data and functions) as separate entities. That is, real world objects are not (usually) merely data nor merely functions. Real world objects instead have both "state" and "behaviors." For instance, people have state (tall, short, etc.) and behavior (playing basketball, running, etc.), often both at the same time, and, of course, in the same person.

Real world objects have states and behaviors.

The aim of object-oriented programming is to imitate this in terms of software, so that "objects" in software have two entities attached to them, states and behavior. This makes the conceptual leap from real-world to programs (hopefully) less of a leap and more of a step. As a result, we can more easily implement ideas into instructions a computer can understand.

7.1.2 The nuts and bolts of objects

What do objects consist of? An object in programming is an entity or "variable" that has two entities attached to it: data and things that act on that data. The data are called attributes of the object, and the functions attached to the object that can act on the data are called methods of the object. Importantly, you *design* these methods to act on the attributes; they aren't random functions someone has attached to the object. In contrast, in procedural programming, variables have only one set of data, the value of the variable, with no functions attached to the variable.

Objects are made up of attributes and methods.

How are objects defined? In the real world, objects are usually examples or specific realizations of some class or type. For instance, individual people are specific realizations of the class of human beings. The specific realizations, or instances, differ from one another in details but have the same pattern. For people, we all have the same general shape, organ structure, etc. In OOP, the specific realizations are called object **instances,** while the common pattern is called a **class.** In Python, this common pattern or template is defined by the `class` statement.

Object instances are specific realizations of a class.

So, in summary, objects are made up of attributes and methods, the structure of a common pattern for a set of objects is called its class, and specific realizations of that pattern are called "instances of that class."

Recall that all the Python "variables" we introduced earlier are actually objects. (In fact, basically everything in Python is an object.) Let's look at a number of different Python objects to illustrate how objects work.

7.2 Example of how objects work: Strings

Python strings (like nearly everything else in Python) are objects. Thus, built into Python, there (implicitly) is a class definition of the string class, and every time you create a string, you are using that definition as your template. That template defines both attributes and methods for all string objects, so whatever string you've created, you have that set of data and functions attached to your string which you can use. Let's look at a specific case:

Example 45 (Viewing attributes and methods attached to strings and trying out a few methods):

In the Python interpreter, type in:

```
a = "hello"
```

Now type: `dir(a)`. What do you see? Type `a.title()` and `a.upper()` and see what you get.

Solution and discussion: The `dir(a)` command gives a list of (nearly) all the attributes and methods attached to the object `a`, which is the string `"hello"`. Note that there is more data attached to the object than just the word "hello", e.g., the attributes `a.__doc__` and `a.__class__` also show up in the `dir` listing.

Methods can act on the data in the object. Thus, `a.title()` applies the `title` method to the data of `a` and returns the string `"hello"` in title case (i.e., the first letter of the word capitalized); `a.upper()` applies the `upper` method to the data of `a` and returns the string all in uppercase. Notice these methods do not require additional input arguments between the parenthesis, because all the data needed is already in the object (i.e., `"hello"`).

The `dir` command shows an object's attributes and methods.

7.3. EXERCISE ON HOW OBJECTS WORK: STRINGS

Review of syntax for objects. Let's do a quick review of syntax for objects. First, to refer to attributes or methods of an instance, you add a period after the object name and then put the attribute or method name. To set an attribute, the reference should be on the lefthand side of the equal sign; the opposite is the case to read an attribute. Method calls require you to have parentheses after the name, with or without arguments, just like a function call. Finally, methods can produce a return value (like a function), act on attributes of the object in-place, or both.

7.3 Exercise on how objects work: Strings

▷ **Exercise 20 (Strings and how objects work):**
In the Python interpreter, type in:

```
a = 'The rain in Spain.'
```

Given string a:

1. Create a new string b that is a but all in uppercase.

2. Is a changed when you create b?

3. How would you test to see whether b is in uppercase? That is, how could you return a boolean that is `True` or `False` depending on whether b is uppercase?

4. How would you calculate the number of occurrences of the letter "n" in a?

The upper, isupper, and count string methods.

Solution and discussion: Here are my solutions:

1. `b = a.upper()`

2. No, the `upper` method's return value is used to create b; the value of a is not changed in place.

3. Use the `isupper` method on the string object, i.e., `b.isupper()` will return `True` or `False`, accordingly.

4. `a.count('n')`

7.4 Example of how objects work: Arrays

While lists have their uses, in scientific computing, arrays are the central object. Most of our discussion of arrays has focused on functions that create and act on arrays. Arrays, however, are objects like any other object and have attributes and methods built-in to them; arrays are more than just a sequence of numbers. Let's look at an example list of all the attributes and methods of an array object:

Example 46 (Examining array object attributes and methods):
In the Python interpreter, type in:

```
a = N.reshape(N.arange(12), (4,3))
```

Now type: `dir(a)`. What do you see? Based on their names, and your understanding of what arrays are, what do you think some of these attributes and methods do?

Solution and discussion: The `dir` command should give you a list of a lot of stuff. I'm not going to list all the output here but instead will discuss the output in general terms.

We first notice that there are two types of attribute and method names: those with double-underscores in front and in back of the name and those without any pre- or post-pended double-underscores. We consider each type of name in turn.

A very few double-underscore names sound like data. The `a.__doc__` variable is one such attribute and refers to documentation of the object. Most of the double-underscore names suggest operations on or with arrays (e.g., add, div, etc.), which is what they are: Those names are of the methods of the array object that *define* what Python will do to your data when the interpreter sees a "+", "/", etc. Thus, if you want to redefine how operators operate on arrays, *you can do so*. It is just a matter of redefining that method of the object.

Double-underscore attribute and method names.

That being said, I do not, in general, recommend you do so. In Python, the double-underscore in front means that attribute or method is "very private." (A variable with a single underscore in front is private, but not as private as a double-underscore variable.) That is to say, it is an attribute or method that normal users should not access, let alone redefine. Python does not, however, do much to prevent you from doing so, so advanced users who need to access or redefine those attributes and methods can do so.

Single-underscore attribute and method names.

7.4. EXAMPLE OF HOW OBJECTS WORK: ARRAYS

Public attributes and methods. The non-double-underscore names are names of "public" attributes and methods, i.e., attributes and methods normal users are expected to access and (possibly) redefine. A number of the methods and attributes of `a` are duplicates of functions (or the output of functions) that act on arrays (e.g., `transpose`, `T`), so you can use either the method version or the function version.

And now let's look at some examples of accessing and using array object attributes and methods:

Example 47 (Using array attributes and methods):
In the Python interpreter, type in:

```
a = N.reshape(N.arange(12), (4,3))
print a.astype('c')
print a.shape
print a.cumsum()
print a.T
```

What do each of the `print` lines do? Are you accessing an attribute or method of the array?:

Solution and discussion: The giveaway as to whether we are accessing attributes or calling methods is whether there are parenthesis after the name; if not, it's an attribute, otherwise, it's a method. Of course, you could type the name of the method without parentheses following, but then the interpreter would just say you specified the method itself, as you did not *call* the method:

How to tell whether you are accessing an attribute or a method.

```
>>> print a.astype
<built-in method astype of numpy.ndarray object at
    0x20d5100>
```

(I manually added a linebreak in the above screenshot to fit it on the page.) That is to say, the above syntax prints the method itself; since you can't meaningfully print the method itself, Python's `print` command just says "this is a method."

The `astype` call produces a version of array `a` that converts the values of `a` into single-character strings. The `shape` attribute gives the shape of the array. The cumsum method returns a flattened version of the array where each element is the cumulative sum of all the elements before. Finally, the attribute T is the transpose of the array a.

Object versions of astype, shape, and cumsum.

While it's nice to have a bunch of array attributes and methods attached to the array object, in practice, I find I seldom access array attributes and find it easier to use NumPy functions instead of the corresponding array methods. One exception with regards to attributes is the `dtype.char` attribute; that's very useful since it tells you the type of the elements of the array (see Example 30 for more on `dtype.char`).

7.5 Exercise on how objects work: Arrays

▷ **Exercise 21 (More on using array attributes and methods):**
For all these exercises (except for the first one), do not use NumPy module functions; only use attributes or methods attached to the arrays. (Do these in order, since each builds on the preceding commands.)

1. Create a 3 column, 4 row *floating point* array named a. The array can have any numerical values you want, as long as all the elements are not all identical.

2. Create an array b that is a copy of a but is 1-D, not 2-D.

3. Turn b into a 6 column, 2 row array, *in place*.

4. Create an array c where you round all elements of b to 1 decimal place.

Solution and discussion: Here are array methods that one can use to accomplish the exercises:

The reshape, ravel, resize, and round function and methods.

1. `a = N.reshape(N.arange(12, dtype='f'), (3,4))`

2. `b = a.ravel()`

3. `b.resize((2,6))`

4. `c = b.round(1)`

7.6. DEFINING YOUR OWN CLASS

Remember, methods need to be called or else they don't do anything; including the parentheses to specify the calling argument list tells the interpreter you're calling the method. In terms of the "output" of the method, some methods act like a function, returning their output as a return value. Other methods do their work "in-place," on the object the method is attached to; those methods do not typically have a return value.[1] The `resize` method is an example of a method that operates on the data in-place, which is why there is no equal sign (for assignment) associated with the method call. You can also make a method operate on an object in-place as well as output a return value.

7.6 Defining your own class

We had said that all objects are instances of a class, and in the preceding examples, we looked at what made up string and array instances, which tells us something about the class definitions for those two kinds of objects. How would we go about creating our own class definitions?

Defining a class using `class`. Class definitions start with `class` statement. The block following the `class` line is the class definition. Within the definition, you refer to the instance of the class as `self`. So, for example, the instance attribute `data` is called `self.data` in the class definition, and the instance method named `calculate` is called `self.calculate` in the class definition (i.e., it is called by `self.calculate()`, if it does not take any arguments).

Defining methods and the `self` argument. Methods are defined using the `def` statement. The first argument in any method is `self`; this syntax is how Python tells a method "make use of all the previously defined attributes and methods in this instance." However, you never type `self` when you call the method.

The `__init__` method. Usually, the first method you define will be the `__init__` method. This method is called whenever you create an instance of the class, and so you usually put code that handles the arguments present when you create (or instantiate) an instance of a class and conducts any kind of initialization for the object instance. The arguments list of `__init__` is the list of arguments passed in to the constructor of the class, which is called when you use the class name with calling syntax.

Whew! This is all very abstract. We need an example! Here's one:

---

[1] This statement is not entirely correct. If you do set another variable, by assignment, to such a method call, that lefthand-side variable will typically be set to None.

7.6. DEFINING YOUR OWN CLASS

Example 48 (Example of a class definition for a Book class):
This class provides a template for holding and manipulating information about a book. The class definition provides a single method (besides the initialization method) that returns a formatted bibliographic reference for the book. The code below gives the class definition and then creates two instances of the class (note line continuations are added to fit the code on the page):

```
1   class Book(object):
2       def __init__(self, authorlast, authorfirst, \
3                    title, place, publisher, year):
4           self.authorlast = authorlast
5           self.authorfirst = authorfirst
6           self.title = title
7           self.place = place
8           self.publisher = publisher
9           self.year = year
10
11      def write_bib_entry(self):
12          return self.authorlast \
13              + ', ' + self.authorfirst \
14              + ', ' + self.title \
15              + ', ' + self.place \
16              + ': ' + self.publisher + ', ' \
17              + self.year + '.'
18
19  beauty = Book( "Dubay", "Thomas" \
20               , "The Evidential Power of Beauty" \
21               , "San Francisco" \
22               , "Ignatius Press", "1999" )
23  pynut = Book( "Martelli", "Alex" \
24               , "Python in a Nutshell" \
25               , "Sebastopol, CA" \
26               , "O'Reilly Media, Inc.", "2003" )
```

Can you explain what each line of code does?

Solution and discussion: Line 1 begins the class definition. By convention, class names follow the CapWords convention (capitalize the first letter of every word). The argument in the class statement is a special object called

The object `object` *and inheritance.*

7.6. DEFINING YOUR OWN CLASS

`object`. This has to do with the OOP idea of inheritance, which is a topic beyond the scope of this book. Suffice it to say that classes you create can inherit or incorporate attributes and methods from other classes. Base classes (class that do not depend on other classes) inherit from `object`, a special object in Python that provides the foundational tools for classes.

Notice how attributes and methods are defined, set, and used in the class definition: Periods separate the instance name `self` from the attribute and method name. So the instance attribute `title` is called `self.title` in the class definition. When you actually create an instance, the instance name is the name of the object (e.g., `beauty`, `pynut`), so the instance attribute `title` of the instance `beauty` is referred to as `beauty.title`, and every instance attribute is separate from every other instance attribute (e.g., `beauty.title` and `pynut.title` are separate variables, not aliases for one another).

Thus, in lines 4–9, I assign each of the positional input parameters in the `def __init__` line to an instance attribute of the same name. Once assigned, these attributes can be used anywhere in the class definition by reference to `self`, as in the definition of the `write_bib_entry` method.

Speaking of which, note that the `write_bib_entry` method is called with no input parameters, but in the class definition in lines 11–17, I still need to provide it with `self` as an input. That way, the method definition is able to make use of all the attributes and methods attached to `self`.

In lines 19–22, I create an instance `beauty` of the `Book` class. Note how the arguments that are passed in are the same arguments as in the `def __init__` argument list. In the last four lines, I create another instance of the `Book` class.

(The code of this example is in *course_files/code_files* in a file called *bibliog.py*.)

Now that we've seen an example of defining a class, let's look at an example of using instances of the `Book` class to help us better understand what this class does:

Example 49 (Using instances of Book):

Consider the `Book` definition given in Example 48. Here are some questions to test your understanding of what it does:

1. How would you print out the `author` attribute of the `pynut` instance (at the interpreter, after running the file)?

2. If you type `print beauty.write_bib_entry()` at the interpreter (after running the file), what will happen?

3. How would you change the publication year for the `beauty` book to `"2010"`?

Solution and discussion: My answers:

1. Type: `print pynut.author`. Remember that once an instance of `Book` is created, the attributes are attached to the actual instance of the class, not to `self`. The only time `self` exists is in the class definition.

2. You will print out the the bibliography formatted version of the information in `beauty`.

3. Type: `beauty.year = "2010"`. Remember that you can change instance attributes of classes you have designed just like you can change instance attributes of any class; just use assignment. (There is also a function called `setattr` that you can use to assign attributes. I'll talk about `setattr` in Section 8.2.)

7.7 Exercise on defining your own class

▷ **Exercise 22 (The Book class and creating an Article class):**
Here are the tasks:

1. Create another instance of the `Book` class using book of your choosing (or make up a book). Execute the `write_bib_entry` method for that instance to check if it looks like what you wanted.

2. Add a method `make_authoryear` to the class definition that will create an attribute `authoryear` and will set that attribute to a string that has the last name of the author and then the year in parenthesis. For instance, for the `beauty` instance, this method will set `authoryear` to `'Dubay (1999)'`. The method *should not have a return statement*.

3. Create an `Article` class that manages information about articles. It will be very similar to the class definition for `Book`, except publisher

7.7. EXERCISE ON DEFINING YOUR OWN CLASS

and place information will be unneeded and article title, volume number, and pages will be needed. Make sure this class also has the methods `write_bib_entry` and `make_authoryear`.

Solution and discussion: Here are my answers:

1. Here's another instance of Book, with a call to the `write_bib_entry` method:

   ```
   madeup = Book("Doe", "John", "Good Book",
                 "Chicago", "Me Press", "2012")
   print madeup.write_bib_entry()
   ```

   This code will print the following to the screen:

   ```
   Doe, John, Good Book, Chicago: Me Press, 2012.
   ```

2. The entire Book class definition, with the new method (and line continuations added to fit the code on the page), is:

   ```
   class Book(object):
       def __init__(self, authorlast, authorfirst, \
                    title, place, publisher, year):
           self.authorlast = authorlast
           self.authorfirst = authorfirst
           self.title = title
           self.place = place
           self.publisher = publisher
           self.year = year

       def make_authoryear(self):
           self.authoryear = self.authorlast \
                           + '(' + self.year +')'

       def write_bib_entry(self):
           return self.authorlast \
                + ', ' + self.authorfirst \
                + ', ' + self.title \
                + ', ' + self.place \
                + ': ' + self.publisher + ', ' \
                + self.year + '.'
   ```

7.7. EXERCISE ON DEFINING YOUR OWN CLASS

The new portion is lines 11–13. None of the rest of the class definition needs to change.

3. The class definition for **Article** (with line continuations added to fit the code on the page) is:

```
 1  class Article(object):
 2      def __init__(self, authorlast, authorfirst, \
 3                   articletitle, journaltitle, \
 4                   volume, pages, year):
 5          self.authorlast = authorlast
 6          self.authorfirst = authorfirst
 7          self.articletitle = articletitle
 8          self.journaltitle = journaltitle
 9          self.volume = volume
10          self.pages = pages
11          self.year = year
12  
13      def make_authoryear(self):
14          self.authoryear = self.authorlast \
15                          + ' (' + self.year +')'
16  
17      def write_bib_entry(self):
18          return self.authorlast \
19              + ', ' + self.authorfirst \
20              + ' (' + self.year + '): ' \
21              + '"' + self.articletitle + ',"' \
22              + self.journaltitle + ', ' \
23              + self.volume + ', ' \
24              + self.pages + '.'
```

This code looks nearly the same as that for the **Book** class, with these exceptions: some attributes differ between the two classes (books, for instance, do not have journal titles) and the method `write_bib_entry` is different between the two classes (to accommodate the different formatting between article and book bibliography entries). See *bibliog.py* in *course_files/code_files* for the code.

7.8 Making classes work together to make complex programming easier

Summary of introduction to OOP. So in our introduction to object-oriented programming (OOP), we found out that objects hold attributes (data) and methods (functions that act on data) together in one related entity. Realizations of an object are called instances. The template or form for an object is called a class, so realizations are instances of a class. In Python, the `class` statement defines the template for object instances. In the `class` statement, instances of the class are called `self`. Once a real instance of the class is created, the instance (object) name itself is "substituted" in for `self`.

But so what? It seems like classes are just a different way of organizing data and functions: Instead of putting them in libraries (or modules), you put them in a class. If you're thinking that this isn't that big of a deal, I would agree that it isn't a big deal, if all you do in a program is write a single class with a single instance of that class; in that case, OOP does not buy you very much.

The real power of OOP, rather, comes when objects are used in conjunction with other classes. By properly designing your set of classes, the object-oriented structure can make your code much simpler to write and understand, easier to debug, and less prone to error. In the remaining sections of the chapter, we'll look at two case studies illustrating the use of OOP in this manner. The first case study extends our `Book` and `Article` classes by examining the more general program of how to create a bibliography. In the second case study, we consider how to create a class for geosciences work that "manages" a surface domain.

7.9 Case study 1: The bibliography example

The `Book` and `Article` classes we wrote earlier manage information related to books and articles. In this case study, we make use of `Book` and `Article` to help us implement one common use of book and article information: the creation of a bibliography. In particular, we'll write a `Bibliography` class that will manage a bibliography, given instances of `Book` and `Article` objects.

7.9.1 Structuring the `Bibliography` class

Since a bibliography consists of a list of (usually formatted) book and article entries, we will want our `Bibliography` class to contain such a list. Thus,

7.9. CASE STUDY 1: THE BIBLIOGRAPHY EXAMPLE

the `Bibliography` class has, as its main attribute, a list of entries which are instances of `Book` and `Article` classes. Remember, instances of `Book` and `Article` can be thought of as books and articles; the instances are the "objects" that specific books and articles are.

Next, we write methods for `Bibliography` that can manipulate the list of `Book` and `Article` instances. To that end, the first two methods we write for `Bibliography` will do the following: initialize an instance of the class; rearrange the list alphabetically based upon last name then first name. The initialization method is called `__init__` (as always), and the rearranging method will be called `sort_entries_alpha`. Here is the code:

```
1   import operator
2
3   class Bibliography(object):
4       def __init__(self, entrieslist):
5           self.entrieslist = entrieslist
6
7       def sort_entries_alpha(self):
8           tmp = sorted(self.entrieslist,
9                    key=operator.attrgetter('authorlast',
10                                            'authorfirst'))
11          self.entrieslist = tmp
12          del tmp
```

Let's talk about what this code does. In the `__init__` method, there is only a single argument, `entrieslist`. This is the list of `Book` and `Article` instances that are being passed into an instance of the `Bibliography` class. The `__init__` method assigns the `entrieslist` argument to an attribute of the same name.

Lines 7–12 define the `sort_entries_alpha` method, which sorts the `entrieslist` attribute and replaces the old `entrieslist` attribute with the sorted version. The method uses the built-in `sorted` function, which takes a keyword parameter `key` that gives the key used for sorting the argument of `sorted`.

How is that key generated? The `attrgetter` function, which is part of the `operator` module, gets the attributes of the names listed as arguments to `attrgetter` out of the elements of the item being sorted. (Note that the attribute names passed into `attrgetter` are strings, and thus you refer to the attributes of interest by their string names, not by typing in their names. This makes the program much easier to write.) In our example, `attrgetter` has two arguments; `sorted` indexes `self.entrieslist` by the `attrgetter`'s first argument attribute name first then the second.

The `attrgetter` function and `sorted`.

7.9. CASE STUDY 1: THE BIBLIOGRAPHY EXAMPLE

Note that at the end of the `sort_entries_alpha` method definition, I use the `del` command to make sure that `tmp` disappears. I need to do this because lists are mutable, and Python assignment is by reference not value (see p. 140 for more discussion on reference vs. value). If I do not remove `tmp`, the `tmp` might float around as a reference to the `entrieslist` attribute; it shouldn't, but I'm paranoid so I explicitly deallocate `tmp` to make sure.

Some final comments: First, if you would like to read more on sorting in Python, please see http://wiki.python.org/moin/HowTo/Sorting. The `sorted` function is very versatile.

Second, there are some diagnostics at the end of *bibliog.py* that are run if you type:

```
python bibliog.py
```

Basic testing of programs. from the operating system command line. This is one way of writing a very basic test to make sure that a module works. (Python has a solid unit testing framework in the form of the unittest module, if you're interested in something more robust.) These diagnostics, however, are not implemented if you import *bibliog.py* as a module. This is due to the conditional:

```
if __name__ == '__main__':
```

which is true only if the module is being run as a main program, i.e., by the `python` command. If you import the module for use in another module, by using `import`, the variable `__name__` will not have the string value `'__main__'`, and the diagnostics will not execute.

7.9.2 What `sort_entries_alpha` illustrates about OOP

Let's pause to think for a moment about the method `sort_entries_alpha`. What have we just done? First, we sorted a list of items that are totally differently structured from each other based on two shared types of data (attributes). Second, we did the sort using a sorting function that does not care about the details of the items being sorted, only that they had these two shared types of data. In other words, the sorting function doesn't care about the source type (e.g., article, book), only that all source types have the attributes `authorlast` and `authorfirst`.

Comparing OOP vs. procedural for a sorting example. This doesn't seem that big a deal, but think about how we would have had to do it in traditional procedural programming. First, each instance would have been an array, with a label of what kind of source it is, for instance:

```
nature_array = ["article", "Smith", "Jane",
                "My Nobel prize-winning paper",
                "Nature", "481", "234-236", "2012"]
```

The procedural sorting function you'd write would need know which elements you want to sort with (here the second and third elements of the array). *But the index for every array of data would potentially be different,* depending on where in the array that data is stored for that source type. Thus, in your sorting function, you'd need to run multiple `if` tests (based on the source type) to extract the correct field in the array to sort by. But, if you changed the key you're sorting by (e.g., from the author's name to the date of publication), you would have to *change the element index you're sorting against.* This means manually changing the code of the `if` tests in your sorting function.

It's easy to make such a manual code change and test that the change works, if you only have a few source types (e.g., articles and books), but what if you have tens or hundreds of source types? What a nightmare! And as you make all those code changes, think of the number of possible bugs you may introduce just from keystroke errors alone! But in object-oriented programming, you can switch the sorting key at will and have an infinite number of source types *without any additional code changes* (e.g., no `if` tests to change). This is the power of OOP over procedural programming: code structured using an OOP framework naturally results in programs that are much more flexible and extensible, resulting in dramatically fewer bugs.

7.9.3   Exercise in extending the `Bibliography` class

▷ **Exercise 23 (Writing out an alphabetically sorted bibliography):**
Since we programmed `Book` and `Article` with `write_bib_entry` methods, let's take advantage of that. Write a method `write_bibliog_alpha` for the `Bibliography` class we just created that actually writes out a bibliography (as a string) with blank lines between the entries, with the entries sorted alphabetically by author name. The bibliography should be returned using a `return` statement in the method. Some hints:

- Elements of a list do not have to all have the same type.

- `for` loops do not only loop through lists of numbers but through any iterable. This includes lists of *any sort*, including lists of objects (such as `Book` and `Article` instances.

- Strings are immutable, so you cannot append to an existing string. Instead, do a reassignment combined with concatenation (i.e., a=a+b).

7.9. CASE STUDY 1: THE BIBLIOGRAPHY EXAMPLE

- To initialize a string, in order to grow it in concatenation steps such as in a `for` loop, start by setting the string variable to an empty string (which is just ' ').

Solution and discussion: Here is the solution for the entire class, with the new method included:

```
1  import operator
2
3  class Bibliography(object):
4      def __init__(self, entrieslist):
5          self.entrieslist = entrieslist
6
7      def sort_entries_alpha(self):
8          tmp = sorted(self.entrieslist,
9                  key=operator.attrgetter('authorlast',
10                                          'authorfirst'))
11         self.entrieslist = tmp
12         del tmp
13
14     def write_bibliog_alpha(self):
15         self.sort_entries_alpha()
16         output = ''
17         for ientry in self.entrieslist:
18             output = output \
19                     + ientry.write_bib_entry() + '\n\n'
20         return output[:-2]
```

The only code that has changed compared to what we had previously is the `write_bibliog_alpha` method; let's talk about what it does. Line 14 defines the method; because `self` is the only argument, the method is called with an empty argument list. The next line calls the `sort_entries_alpha` method to make sure the list that is stored in the `entrieslist` attribute is alphabetized. Next, we initialize the output string `output` as an empty string. When the "+" operator is used, Python will then use string concatenation on it. Lines 17–19 run a `for` loop to go through all elements in the list `entrieslist`. The output of `write_bib_entry` is added one entry at a time, along with two linebreaks after it. Finally, the entire string is output except for the final two linebreaks. (Remember that strings can be manipulated using list slicing syntax.)

7.9.4 What the `write_bibliog_alpha` method illustrates about OOP

Here too, let's ask how would we have written a function that wrote out an alphabetized bibliography in procedural programming? Probably something like the following sketch:

```
def write_bibliog_function(arrayofentries):
    [open output file]

    for i in xrange(len(arrayofentries)):
        ientryarray = arrayofentries[i]
        if ientryarray[0] = "article":
            [call function for bibliography entry
              for an article, and save to output file]
        elif ientryarray[0] == "book":
            [call function for bibliography entry
              for an book, and save to output file]
        [...]

    [close output file]
```

This solution sketch illustrates how in procedural programming we are stuck writing `if` tests in the bibliography writing function to make sure we format each source entry correctly, depending on source type (e.g., article, book). In fact, for *every* function that deals with multiple source types, we need this tree of `if` tests. If you introduce another source type, you need to add another `if` test in *all functions* where you have this testing tree. This is a recipe for disaster: It is exceedingly easy to inadvertently add an `if` test in one function but forget to do so in another function, etc.

In contrast, with objects, adding another source type *requires no code changes or additions*. The new source type just needs a `write_bib_entry` method defined for it. And, since methods are *designed* to work with the attributes of their class, this method will be tailor-made for its data. So much easier!

7.10 Case study 2: Creating a class for geosciences work—Surface domain management

I think the bibliography example in Section 7.9 does a good job of illustrating what object-oriented programming gives you that procedural programming

7.10. CASE STUDY 2: CREATING A CLASS FOR GEOSCIENCES WORK—SURFACE DOMAIN MANAGEMENT

cannot. I also like the example because all of us have had to write a bibliography, and the idea of "sources" (books, articles) very nicely lends itself to being thought of as an "object." But can the OOP way of thinking help us in decomposing a geosciences problem? In this section, we consider a class for managing surface domains (i.e., a latitude-longitude domain). I present the task of defining the class as an exercise and give two possible solutions. The exercise and solutions, while valuable in and of themselves, offer a nice illustration of how OOP enables atmospheric and oceanic scientists to write more concise but flexible code for handling scientific calculations.

Science Publication Hell

▷ **Exercise 24 (Defining a `SurfaceDomain` class):**

Define a class `SurfaceDomain` that describes surface domain instances. The domain is a land or ocean surface region whose spatial extent is described by a latitude-longitude grid. The class is instantiated when you provide a vector of longitudes and latitudes; the surface domain is a regular grid based on these vectors. Surface parameters (e.g., elevation, temperature, roughness, etc.) can then be given as instance attributes. The quantities are given on the domain grid.

In addition, in the class definition, provide an **instantiation** method that saves the input longitude and latitude vectors as appropriately named attributes and creates 2-D arrays of the shape of the domain grid which have the longitude and latitude values at each point and saves them as private attributes (i.e., their names begin with a single underscore).

7.10. CASE STUDY 2: CREATING A CLASS FOR GEOSCIENCES WORK—SURFACE DOMAIN MANAGEMENT

Hint: An example may help with regards to what I'm asking for with respect to the 2-D arrays. If `lon=N.arange(5)` and `lat=N.arange(4)`, then the `_lonall` instance attribute would be:

```
[[0 1 2 3 4]
 [0 1 2 3 4]
 [0 1 2 3 4]
 [0 1 2 3 4]]
```

and the `_latall` instance attribute would be:

```
[[0 0 0 0 0]
 [1 1 1 1 1]
 [2 2 2 2 2]
 [3 3 3 3 3]]
```

Solution and discussion: The two solutions described below (with the second solution commented out) are in *course_files/code_files* in the file *surface_domain.py*). Here's the solution using **for** loops:

```
import numpy as N

class SurfaceDomain(object):
    def __init__(self, lon, lat):
        self.lon = N.array(lon)
        self.lat = N.array(lat)

        shape2d = (N.size(self.lat), N.size(self.lon))
        self._lonall = N.zeros(shape2d, dtype='f')
        self._latall = N.zeros(shape2d, dtype='f')
        for i in xrange(shape2d[0]):
            for j in xrange(shape2d[1]):
                self._lonall[i,j] = self.lon[j]
                self._latall[i,j] = self.lat[i]
```

Lines 5–6 guarantee that `lon` and `lat` are NumPy arrays, in case lists or tuples are passed in.

And here's a simpler and faster solution using the `meshgrid` function in NumPy instead of the **for** loops:

Using meshgrid.

7.10. CASE STUDY 2: CREATING A CLASS FOR GEOSCIENCES WORK—SURFACE DOMAIN MANAGEMENT

```
1   import numpy as N
2
3   class SurfaceDomain(object):
4       def __init__(self, lon, lat):
5           self.lon = N.array(lon)
6           self.lat = N.array(lat)
7           [xall, yall] = N.meshgrid(self.lon, self.lat)
8           self._lonall = xall
9           self._latall = yall
10          del xall, yall
```

So, what does this `SurfaceDomain` class illustrate about OOP applied to the geosciences? Pretend you have multiple `SurfaceDomain` instances that you want to communicate to each other, where the bounds of one are taken from (or interpolated with) the bounds of another, e.g., calculations for each domain instance are farmed out to a separate processor, and you're stitching domains together:

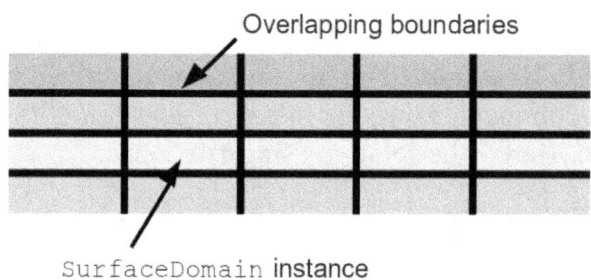

In the above schematic, gray areas are `SurfaceDomain` instances and the thick, dark lines are the overlapping boundaries between the domain instances.

Comparing OOP vs. procedural for a subdomain management example.

In procedural programming, to manage this set of overlapping domains, you might create a grand domain encompassing all points in all the domains to make an index that keeps track of which domains abut one another. The index records who contributes data to these boundary regions. Alternately, you might create a function that processes only the neighboring domains, but this function will be called from a scope that has access to all the domains (e.g., via a common block).

But, to manage this set of overlapping domains, you don't really need such a global view nor access to all domains. In fact, a global index or a common block means that if you change your domain layout, you have to hand-code a change to your index/common block. Rather, what you actually need is only to be able to interact with your neighbor. So why not just write a method that takes *your neighboring* `SurfaceDomain` *instances as arguments* and alters the boundaries accordingly? That is, why not add the following to the `SurfaceDomain` class definition:[2]

```
class SurfaceDomain(object):
    [...]
    def syncbounds(self, northobj, southobj,
                   eastobj, westobj):
        [...]
```

Such a method will propagate to all `SurfaceDomain` instances automatically, once written in the class definition. Thus, you only have to write one (relatively) small piece of code that can then affect any number of layouts of `SurfaceDomain` instances. Again, object-oriented programming enables you to push the level at which you code to solve a problem down to a lower-level than procedural programming easily allows. As a result, you can write smaller, better tested bit of code; this makes your code more robust and flexible.

7.11 Summary

You could, I think, fairly summarize this chapter as addressing one big question: Why should an atmospheric or oceanic scientist bother with object-oriented programming? In answer, I suggest two reasons. First, code written using OOP is less prone to error. OOP enables you to mostly eliminate lengthy argument lists, and it is much more difficult for a function to accidentally process data it should not process. Additionally, OOP deals with long series of conditional tests much more compactly; there is no need to duplicate `if` tests in multiple places. Finally, objects enable you to test smaller pieces of your program (e.g., individual attributes and methods), which makes your tests more productive and effective.

Second, programs written using OOP are more easily extended. New cases are easily added by creating new classes that have the interface methods defined for them. Additional functionality is also easily added by just adding new methods/attributes. Finally, any changes to class definitions automatically propagate to all instances of the class.

For short, quick-and-dirty programs, procedural programming is still the better option; there is no reason to spend the time coding the additional OOP infrastructure. But for many atmospheric and oceanic sciences applications,

Procedural for short programs; OOP for everything else.

---

[2]Christian Dieterich's PyOM pythonized OM3 ocean model does a similar kind of domain-splitting handling in Python.

7.11. SUMMARY

things can very quickly become complex. As soon as that happens, the object decomposition can really help. Here's the rule-of-thumb I use: For a one-off, short program, I write it procedurally, but for any program I may extend someday (even if it is a tentative "may"), I write it using objects.

Chapter 8

An Introduction to OOP Using Python: Part II—Application to Atmospheric Sciences Problems

Ch. 7, introduced us to the syntax of object-oriented programming (OOP), as well as an understanding of how we can use OOP to write AOS programs that are more flexible, extensible, and less error prone. In this chapter, we look at a few applications of OOP to AOS problems. In particular, we will examine how objects can be used to manage dataset metadata (including missing values), related but unknown data, and dynamically change subroutine execution order. Of these three topics, the first is addressed by two well-developed packages, NumPy and the Climate Data Management System (cdms). The second and third topics are implemented in two experimental packages, but they provide useful illustrations of how we can apply OOP to AOS problems.

8.1 Managing metadata and missing values

All datasets of real-world phenomena will have missing data: instruments will malfunction, people will make measurement errors, etc. Traditionally, missing data has been handled by assigning a value as the "missing value" and setting all elements of the dataset that are "bad" to that value. (Usually, the missing value is a value entirely out of the range of the expected values, e.g., −99999.0.) With OOP, objects enable us to do this in a more robust way.

Earlier, we saw that Python supports array variables (via NumPy), and we also described how all variables in Python are not technically variables, but objects. Objects hold multiple pieces of data as well as functions that

8.1. MANAGING METADATA AND MISSING VALUES

operate on that data, and for atmospheric and oceanic sciences (AOS) applications, this means data and metadata (e.g., grid type, missing values, etc.) can both be attached to the "variable." Using this capability, we can define not only arrays, but two more array-like variables: masked arrays and masked variables. These array-like variables incorporate metadata attached to the arrays and define how that metadata can be used as part of analysis, visualization, etc.

Oceanographic Bullies

8.1.1 What are masked arrays and masked variables?

Recall that arrays are *n*-dimensional vectors or grids that hold numbers (or characters). Masked arrays, then, are arrays that also have a "mask" attribute which tells you which elements are bad, and masked variables are masked arrays that also give domain information and other metadata information. Let's look at each type of variable in detail.

Review of arrays. In an array, every element has a value, and operations using the array are defined accordingly. Thus, for the following array:

```
>>> import numpy as N
>>> a = N.array([[1,2,3],[4,5,6]])
>>> a
array([[1, 2, 3],
       [4, 5, 6]])
```

8.1. MANAGING METADATA AND MISSING VALUES

the contents of the array are numbers, and operations such as addition, multiplication, etc. are defined as operating on those array elements, as we saw in Ch. 4.

Masked arrays are arrays with something extra. That something extra is a mask of bad values; this mask is an attribute of the array and thus automatically travels with the numerical (or character) values of the elements of the array. Elements of the array, whose corresponding elements in the mask are set to "bad," are treated as if they did not exist, and operations using the array automatically utilize the mask of bad values. Consider the array a and the masked array b:

Masked arrays.

```
>>> import numpy as N
>>> import numpy.ma as ma
>>> a = N.array([[1,2,3],[4,5,6]])
>>> b = ma.masked_greater(a, 4)
>>> b
masked_array(data =
 [[1 2 3]
 [4 -- --]],
             mask =
 [[False False False]
 [False  True  True]],
      fill_value = 999999)
>>> print a*b
[[1 4 9]
 [16 -- --]]
```

The mask is a boolean array whose elements are set to **True** if the value in the corresponding array is considered "bad." Thus, in the masked array b, the last two elements of the second row have mask values set to **True**, and when the data for the masked array is printed out for a human viewer, those elements display "--" instead of a number.

Masked array masks.

We also note that the masked array b has an attribute called **fill_value** that is set to 999999. As we'll see in Example 52, this is the value used to fill-in all the "bad" elements when we "deconstruct" the masked array. That is to say, when we convert a masked array to a normal NumPy array, we need to put something in for all the "bad" elements (i.e., where the mask is **True**): the value of **fill_value** is what we put in for the "bad" elements.

Masked array fill values.

Just as operators have been defined to operate in a special way when the operands are arrays (i.e., the + operator adds element-wise for arrays), operators have also been defined to operate in a special way for masked arrays.

8.1. MANAGING METADATA AND MISSING VALUES

```
>>> import MV2
>>> d = MV2.masked_greater(c,4)
>>> d.info()
*** Description of Slab variable_3 ***
id: variable_3
shape: (3, 2)
filename:
missing_value: 1e+20
comments:
grid_name: N/A
grid_type: N/A
time_statistic:
long_name:
units:
No grid present.
** Dimension 1 **
   id: axis_0
   Length: 3
   First:  0.0
   Last:   2.0
   Python id:   0x2729450
[... rest of output deleted for space ...]
```

Metadata {
Axes {

Figure 8.1: Example of information attached to a masked variable. Adapted from a figure by Bob Drach, Dean Williams, and Charles Doutriaux. Used by permission.

Operations using masked arrays.
For masked arrays, operations using elements whose mask value is set to **True** will create results that also have a mask value set to **True**. Thus, in the example above, the product of array **a** and masked array **b** yields an array whose last two elements of the second row are also "bad," since those corresponding elements in masked array **b** are bad: a good value times a bad value gives a bad value. Thus, masked arrays transparently deal with missing data in real-world datasets.

Masked variables.
A masked variable is like a masked array but with additional information, such as axes and domain information, metadata, etc. Figure 8.1 shows an example of the additional information that can be attached to a masked variable.

The domain information and other metadata attached to a masked variable can be used in analysis and visualization routines. UV-CDAT functions, for instance, are pre-built to do just this. As an example, consider Figure 8.2 which shows the use of UV-CDAT's cdms2 module to read in the total cloudiness (clt) variable from a netCDF file and UV-CDAT's vcs module to render the plot using a single command. This is possible because the vcs `boxfill` method uses the information attached to the masked variable to properly title the graph, label the units, etc.

As a summary, Figure 8.3 gives a schematic that shows how each of these three types of "arrays" relate to each other. Arrays and masked arrays are both part of NumPy whereas masked variables are part of UV-CDAT.

8.1. MANAGING METADATA AND MISSING VALUES

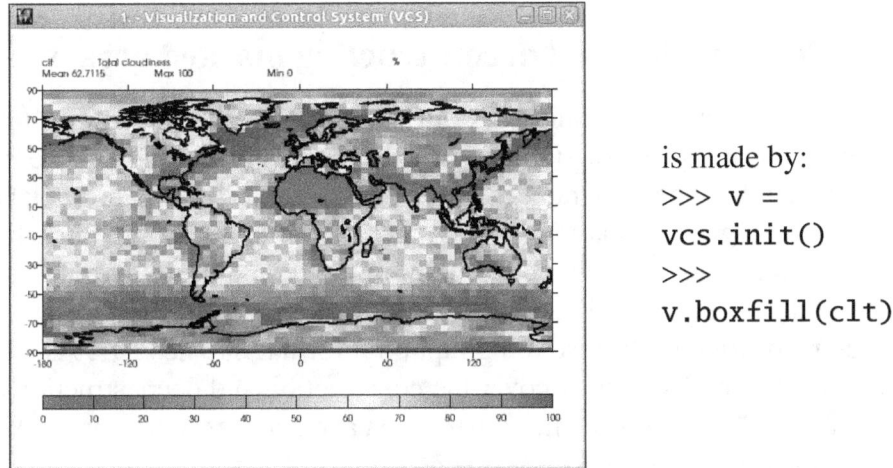

is made by:
```
>>> v = vcs.init()
>>> v.boxfill(clt)
```

Figure 8.2: Example showing plot of the total cloudiness (clt) variable read from a netCDF file and the code used to generate the plot, using UV-CDAT masked variables.

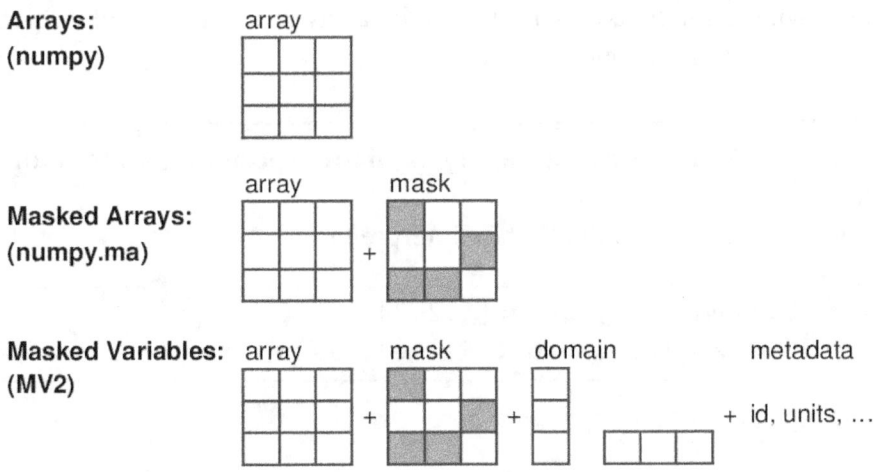

Figure 8.3: Schematic of arrays, masked arrays, and masked variables. Adapted from a drawing by Bob Drach, Dean Williams, and Charles Doutriaux. Used by permission.

8.1. MANAGING METADATA AND MISSING VALUES

(See Section 10.2 for more information on UV-CDAT.)

8.1.2 Constructing and deconstructing masked arrays

We covered construction of normal NumPy arrays in Ch. 4, so we won't revisit that topic here. Construction of masked variables is normally not something you would do in a program; if you already have the metadata available to you in the program, it may not make much sense to attach it to a masked variable instead of using it directly later on in the program. Many times, for most common uses, masked variables will be automatically constructed for you upon read from a self-describing input file format like netCDF. As a result, in this section, I will only cover the construction and deconstruction of masked arrays. For details on the construction and deconstruction of masked variables, please see the CDAT documentation.[1]

Masked array submodule and constructors. NumPy provides a number of masked array constructors. I'll illustrate the use of a few of these constructors through examples. Details of these functions, as well as information on other masked array constructors, are found in the NumPy documentation.[2] In the examples below, all functions are part of the `numpy.ma` submodule and I assume I've already imported that submodule with `import numpy.ma as MA` and that NumPy is already imported as `import numpy as N`. Before you type in the example, try to guess what the output will be, based on the command syntax itself. Note that you can see what a looks like by typing in the array name `a` by itself, which will reveal the data, mask, and fill value.

Example 50 (Make a masked array by explicitly specifying a mask and fill value):

Type in the following in the Python interpreter:

```
a = MA.masked_array(data=[1,2,3],
        mask=[True, True, False], fill_value=1e20)
```

What does the variable `a` look like?

Solution and discussion: As expected, the first two array elements are now considered "bad." Here is the result of an array inquiry done in the Python interpreter:

---

[1] http://www2-pcmdi.llnl.gov/cdat/manuals (accessed August 17, 2012).
[2] http://docs.scipy.org/doc/numpy/reference/maskedarray.html (accessed August 17, 2012).

8.1. MANAGING METADATA AND MISSING VALUES

```
>>> a
masked_array(data = [-- -- 3],
            mask = [ True  True False],
      fill_value = 999999)
```

Often times, we determine which data values should be masked on the basis of whether or not the data values are beyond a given acceptable value or some other similar test. Thus, it makes sense to have functions to create masked arrays based on such tests. Here are a few examples of such functions:

Example 51 (Make a masked array by masking values based on conditions):
Type in the following in the Python interpreter:

```
a = MA.masked_greater([1,2,3,4], 3)
data = N.array([1,2,3,4,5])
b = MA.masked_where(N.logical_and(data>2, data<5), data)
```

Masked array construction using conditions.

What do the variables a and b look like?

Solution and discussion: The first line creates a masked array a where all values greater than 3 have mask values set to **True**. The third line creates a masked array b where all values greater than 2 and less than 5 have mask values set to **True**. Note that `masked_where`'s first argument is a boolean array that specifies where the mask will be set to **True**. An inquiry into masked arrays a and b should return:

```
>>> a
masked_array(data = [1 2 3 --],
            mask = [False False False  True],
      fill_value = 999999)
>>> b
masked_array(data = [1 2 -- -- 5],
            mask = [False False  True  True False],
      fill_value = 999999)
```

There are times when we want just a regular NumPy array—perhaps to output to a file format that does not support object attributes—and so we

8.1. MANAGING METADATA AND MISSING VALUES

Converting from a masked array to a regular array with `filled`.

need a way to convert a masked array into a normal array. In that conversion, the function will fill all "bad" elements with a special value that no "good" element would have. The masked array submodule function `filled` does the job. Let's look at an example:

Example 52 (Make a regular NumPy array from a masked array):
Type in the following in the Python interpreter:

```
b = MA.masked_array(data=[1.0, 2.0, 3.0],
        mask=[True, True, False], fill_value=-1e23)
a = MA.filled(b)
```

What do the variables b and a look like?

Solution and discussion: In this example, we start with a masked array and convert it into a normal NumPy array a. Thus, the variables b and a are:

```
>>> b
masked_array(data = [-- -- 3.0],
            mask = [ True  True False],
        fill_value = -1e+23)
>>> a
array([ -1.00000000e+23,  -1.00000000e+23,
        3.00000000e+00])
```

Customized fill value for a masked array.

(I manually added a line break in the screenshot to make it fit on the page.) Note that we create our masked array with a fill value different than the default of 999999. Thus, the array a that results will have -1×10^{23} as the "missing value" value. Also note that if the type of `data` and the type of `fill_value` conflict, the default value of `fill_value` will be used despite the explicit specification of `fill_value` in the function call (if the default `fill_value` is of the same type as `data`). Thus:

```
>>> b = MA.masked_array(data=[1, 2, 3],
        mask=[True, True, False], fill_value=-1e23)
>>> b
masked_array(data = [-- -- 3],
            mask = [ True  True False],
        fill_value = 999999)
```

yields a masked array b with a `fill_value` set to the default value, which is an integer.

8.1. MANAGING METADATA AND MISSING VALUES

By the way, the `filled` function also comes in a masked array method form, so instead of calling the function `filled`, i.e:

    a = MA.filled(b)

Filled is also a masked array method.

you can call the method attached to the masked array, i.e.:

    a = b.filled()

Remember, *bad values* (i.e., the missing values) have mask values set to `True` in a masked array.

8.1.3 Exercise using masked arrays

▷ **Exercise 25 (Creating and using a masked array of surface air temperature):**

Open the example netCDF NCEP/NCAR Reanalysis 1 netCDF dataset of monthly mean surface/near-surface air temperature (or the netCDF dataset you brought) and read in the values of the `air`, `lat`, and `lon` variables into NumPy arrays. Take *only the first time slice* of the air temperature data. (The example data is in *course_files/datasets* in the file *air.mon.mean.nc*.)

Create an array that masks out temperatures in that time slice in all locations greater than 45°N and less than 45°S. Convert all those temperature values to K (the dataset temperatures are in °C). Some hints:

- You can use the code in *exercise-netcdf.py* in *course_files/code_files* as a starting point.

- Use the `meshgrid` function in NumPy to make it easier to handle the latitude values in array syntax (you can, of course, always use `for` loops).

- The air temperature, directly from the netCDF file, has the shape (755, 73, 144) and thus is dimensioned time, latitude, longitude.

- You can test whether you masked it correctly by printing the values of your masked array at the poles and equator (i.e., if your masked array is called `ma_data`, you would print `ma_data[0,:]`, `ma_data[-1,:]`, and `ma_data[36,:]`).

8.2. MANAGING RELATED BUT UNKNOWN DATA: SEEING IF ATTRIBUTES ARE DEFINED

Solution and discussion: Here's my solution:

```
1   import numpy as N
2   import numpy.ma as MA
3   import Scientific.IO.NetCDF as S
4
5   fileobj = S.NetCDFFile('air.mon.mean.nc', mode='r')
6   data = fileobj.variables['air'].getValue()[0,:,:]
7   lat = fileobj.variables['lat'].getValue()
8   lon = fileobj.variables['lon'].getValue()
9   fileobj.close()
10
11  [lonall, latall] = N.meshgrid(lon, lat)
12  ma_data = MA.masked_where( \
13          N.logical_or(latall>45,latall<-45), data )
14  ma_data = ma_data + 273.15
15
16  print 'North pole:  ', ma_data[0,:]
17  print 'South pole:  ', ma_data[-1,:]
18  print 'Equator:     ', ma_data[36,:]
```

The result of line 16 should show that all the points in the zeroth row of ma_data are "bad," as should the result of line 17 for the last row. All the points in line 18, which are the Equatorial points, should be "good" values, and in units of Kelvin.

See the code in *exercise-ma.py* in *course_files/code_files* for the above solution (with minor changes).

8.2 Managing related but unknown data: Seeing if attributes are defined

In the atmospheric and oceanic sciences, we are often interested in "secondary" quantities, for instance, virtual temperature, vorticity, etc., that are derived from "primary" quantities (like temperature, pressure, etc.) and other secondary quantities. In other words, final quantities often depend on both basic and intermediate quantities. For instance, density depends on virtual temperature which depends on temperature. Thus, many of these quantities are related to each other.

In traditional procedural programming, to calculate secondary variables, we would figure out all the quantities we want to calculate (both final and intermediate), allocate variables for all those quantities, then calculate our desired variables using the proper sequence of functions. But unless we know

8.2. MANAGING RELATED BUT UNKNOWN DATA: SEEING IF ATTRIBUTES ARE DEFINED

exactly what we want to calculate, we won't know what variables to allocate and what functions to call; we often get around that problem by allocating memory for every conceivable variable of interest. But why should we have to do this? Put another way, the problem with the procedural method is that we are limited to *static* analysis. Since computers are all about automation, why can't we have the computer automatically calculate what quantities it needs when it needs it; in the atmosphere and ocean, all these quantities are interrelated. This would enable *dynamic* analysis.

Python, it turns out, can do dynamic variable management. At any time in the program, objects can add and remove attributes and methods and check if an attribute or method exists. Let's take advantage of these capabilities and design a class to manage the multiple atmospheric quantities we're calculating: to make sure we have calculated what we need to calculate, when we need it. We define an object class `Atmosphere` where the following occurs:

Using Python for dynamic variable management.

- Atmospheric quantities are assigned to attributes of instances of the class.

- Methods to calculate atmospheric quantities:

    - Check to make sure the required quantity exists as an attribute.

    - If it doesn't exist, the method is executed to calculate that quantity.

    - After the quantity is calculated, it is set as an attribute of the object instance.

What might something with these traits look like in Python code? Here's a skeleton class definition:

8.2. MANAGING RELATED BUT UNKNOWN DATA: SEEING IF ATTRIBUTES ARE DEFINED

```
1   class Atmosphere(object):
2       def __init__(self, **kwds):
3           for ikey in kwds.keys():
4               setattr(self, ikey, kwds[ikey])
5
6       def calc_rho(self):
7           if not hasattr(self, 'T_v'):
8               self.calc_virt_temp()
9           elif not hasattr(self, 'p'):
10              self.calc_press()
11          else:
12              raise ValueError, \
13                  "cannot obtain given initial quantities"
14
15          self.rho = \
16              [... find air density from self.T_v and
17                  self.p ...]
```

The setattr, hasattr, getattr, and delattr functions. Before talking about the code in specific, let me briefly describe what the setattr, hasattr, getattr, and delattr functions do (the last two are not used in the code above, but I describe them for completeness). As the names suggest, these functions manipulate or inquire of the attributes of objects. However, because they are functions, they enable you to interact with attributes without having to actually type out the name of the attribute. For instance, consider the act of setting an attribute which we've already seen can be done with assignment. So, if we have the following masked array a (as in Example 51):

```
import numpy.ma as MA
a = MA.masked_greater([1,2,3,4], 3)
```

we can manually change the fill value from its default value 999999 to something else by assignment:

```
>>> a.fill_value=-100
>>> a
masked_array(data = [1 -- --],
             mask = [False  True  True],
       fill_value = -100)
```

or we can use the function setattr:

8.2. MANAGING RELATED BUT UNKNOWN DATA: SEEING IF ATTRIBUTES ARE DEFINED

```
>>> setattr(a, 'fill_value', 456)
>>> a
masked_array(data = [1 -- --],
             mask = [False  True  True],
       fill_value = 456)
```

The `setattr` function takes three arguments. The first is the object whose attribute you wish to set. The second is the name of the attribute you wish to set (as a string). The third argument is the new value of the attribute you are setting. Because `setattr` is a function, you can pass in the arguments as variables. You do not have to type in a period and equal sign, which the assignment syntax requires you to do. Functions can receive variables as arguments and so can be automated; typing a period and equal sign can only be applied to actually defined objects and so cannot be automated. Normally, methods are tailored for a class of objects and will not be set during run-time. However, you can add methods to an instance at run-time, if you wish, by setting an attribute to a function or method object.

The `hasattr` function tests whether a given object has an attribute or method of a given name. It takes two arguments, the first being the object under inquiry and the second being the name of the attribute or method you're checking for, as a string. `True` is returned if the object has the attribute you're checking for, `False` otherwise. Thus, for masked array a:

```
a = MA.masked_greater([1,2,3,4], 3)
print hasattr(a, 'fill_value')
print hasattr(a, 'foobar')
```

the first `print` line will print `True` while the second will print `False`.

The functions `getattr` and `delattr` have the same syntax: The first argument is the object in question while the second argument is the attribute to either get or delete. `getattr` returns the attribute or method of interest while `delattr` removes the attribute of interest from the given object. (Note that `delattr` cannot remove a method that is hard-coded into the class definition.)

With this as background, let's see what this code does. We pass in initial values for our atmospheric variables via the `__init__` method, as normal, but in this case, all our initial values come through keyword parameters as given in the `kwds` dictionary (see Example 16 for more on passing a keyword parameters dictionary into a function, as opposed to referring to every keyword parameter manually). In our keyword parameters dictionary, we assume that the keyword names will be the names of the attributes that store those parameter values. Once passed in we set the keyword parameters to instance

8.2. MANAGING RELATED BUT UNKNOWN DATA: SEEING IF ATTRIBUTES ARE DEFINED

attributes of the same name as the keyword. For instance, if an `Atmosphere` object is instantiated by:

```
myatmos = Atmosphere(T=data1, q=data2)
```

(where `data1` and `data2` are the data, most likely arrays), then upon instantiation, `myatmos` will have the attribute `T` and the attribute `q` which refer to the data variables `data1` and `data2`, respectively. That is to say, `myatmos.T` refers to the `data1` data while `myatmos.q` refers to the `data2` data.

How does the `__init__` code do this? In lines 3–4 in the class definition, we loop through the keys in `kwds`, which are strings, and use the built-in function `setattr` to set the values of the dictionary entries to attributes of the instance (i.e., `self`), with the names given by the corresponding keys (i.e., `ikey`). Note how *we do not have to type in the variables to set them!* The function `setattr` does this for us. Thus, in our class definition, we do not need to know ahead of time which atmospheric quantities will be initially defined; all that can be determined at **runtime,** and our code will be the same.

How do methods that calculate quantities work with the attributes that hold atmospheric data? Lines 6–17 in the class definition define the method `calc_rho` which calculates air density using an algorithm that requires virtual temperature and pressure be already defined. So, `calc_rho` first checks if those attributes exist (the built-in `hasattr` function checks to see if an attribute is defined in the instance `self`), and if not, `calc_rho` calls the methods (defined elsewhere in the class) that calculate those atmospheric quantities. Those methods, in turn, are structured just like `calc_rho` and will do the same thing (check for an atmospheric quantity attribute, and if not found, calculate that quantity). Eventually, you'll calculate what you need given what you have; if not, you'll get an error (as in the `raise` statement of lines 12–13). Once all necessary variables are calculated, lines 16–17 calculates the air density and line 15 sets the result to an instance attribute of `self` called `rho`.

So, let's step back and think about what we've just done. First, because the class `Atmosphere` stores all primary and secondary atmospheric quantities needed to arrive at a quantity of interest, and the algorithms of `Atmosphere` are (hopefully) consistent with each other, all of the atmospheric quantities in an `Atmosphere` instance will be consistent with one another. Second, by using the `hasattr` function, the class automatically ensures all necessary secondary quantities are available if needed for the current calculation. In fact, the class *will find a way* to calculate what you asked it to, if the algorithms in the class will allow you to make the calculation you want using the initial values you gave. Lastly, the class can be used with any set of initial values that are input. The ability to inquire of and manipulate the attributes and methods of an object through functions enables us to write code in which the names of the initial atmospheric quantities are not known ahead of time. Our code is more flexible (and, in this case, concise) as a result.

8.3 Exercise to add to the Atmosphere class

▷ **Exercise 26 (Adding the method `calc_virt_temp`):**
Write the skeleton definition for a method `calc_virt_temp` (to be added to the `Atmosphere` class) that calculates the virtual temperature given mixing ratio (`r`) and temperature (`T`). Have this method call a method to calculate mixing ratio (`calc_mix_ratio`) if mixing ratio is not yet an object attribute. (We'll assume temperature has to be given.)

Solution and discussion: Here's the `Atmosphere` class with the skeleton definition for `calc_virt_temp` added:

8.3. EXERCISE TO ADD TO THE ATMOSPHERE CLASS

```
1   class Atmosphere(object):
2       def __init__(self, **kwds):
3           for ikey in kwds.keys():
4               setattr(self, ikey, kwds[ikey])
5
6       def calc_rho(self):
7           if not hasattr(self, 'T_v'):
8               self.calc_virt_temp()
9           elif not hasattr(self, 'p'):
10              self.calc_press()
11          else:
12              raise ValueError, \
13                  "cannot obtain given initial quantities"
14
15          self.rho = \
16              [... find air density using self.T_v and
17                  self.p ...]
18
19      def calc_virt_temp(self):
20          if not hasattr(self, 'r'):
21              self.calc_mix_ratio()
22          else:
23              raise ValueError, \
24                  "cannot obtain given initial quantities"
25
26          self.T_v = \
27              [... find virtual temperature using
28                  self.r and self.T ...]
```

I once wrote a package atmqty that does what **Atmosphere** does. It was one of the earlier things I wrote and needs a major rewrite, but you might find some of the routines and the structure to be informative.[3] Also, the object-oriented approach **Atmosphere** uses was essentially the way R. Saravanan in the late 1990's (then at NCAR) structured his Hyperslab OPerator Suite (HOPS) toolkit for manipulating climate model output. Written for the Interactive Data Language (IDL) and Yorick, Saravanan's work was really ahead of its time in the atmospheric and oceanic sciences community.[4]

One final note: In this section, we discussed dynamic variable management via object attributes and methods. But this may sound familiar to you—

---

[3] See http://www.johnny-lin.com/py_pkgs/atmqty/doc for details (accessed August 17, 2012).

[4] See http://www.cgd.ucar.edu/cdp/svn/hyperslab.html for details (accessed April 5, 2012).

aren't these the same things that a dictionary can do? Through this example, we've stumbled upon a secret in Python. Not only is everything an object in Python, but (nearly) everything in Python is managed by dictionaries. All objects have a private attribute `__dict__`, a data structure that manages the attributes and methods namespace just like a dictionary because it is a dictionary! And so, if you really need to, you can access that dictionary like any other dictionary. (I do not, however, recommend this.)[5] This is a nice illustration of how compact is the definition of Python: a relatively small set of data structures and principles are repeatedly reused in many aspects of the language's definition. This makes the language easier to use, because you have fewer "special structures" to try and remember.

> Nearly everything in Python is managed by dictionaries.

8.4 Dynamically changing subroutine execution order (optional)

(This section is a bit more advanced, so if you feel like it's a little too much, just skip it. The main idea is that by using lists and an object encapsulation, you can dynamically change subroutine execution order in a Python program. This opens up AOS models to easily answer whole new classes of scientific problems.)

In traditional procedural programming, the execution order of subroutines is fixed, because subroutines are called by typing in the subroutine name (along with a `call` statement, in Fortran). Even branching (via `if` statements) is fixed in that the node cannot move from the place where you typed it in.

> In procedural programming, subroutine execution order is fixed.

In contrast, we saw that Python's list structure is an ordered set that is mutable and can be changed *while the program is running*. Why, then, don't we use a list to manage subroutine execution order? Then, if we want to alter execution order, we just reorder, insert, and/or delete elements from the list.

We'll embed such a list of subroutines—a "runlist"—as an attribute of the same name in a class `Model` where each of the subroutines is a method of the class and a method `execute_runlist` will go through the list of subroutines, executing them in order. A skeleton definition for such a class, for an oceanic general circulation model (GCM), might look like the following

> Python lists are runtime mutable. Use them to manage subroutine execution order.

---

[5] In general, you would do well to limit your interaction with `__dict__` to the built-in functions (e.g., `hasattr`) designed for such interactions. I confess, in my earlier days in using Python, I wrote a lot of code that directly accessed `__dict__`, but I now repent of what I did.

8.4. DYNAMICALLY CHANGING SUBROUTINE EXECUTION ORDER (OPTIONAL)

(note the runlist is not a complete listing of all routines in the model, but I list just a few to illustrate the idea):

```
1   class Model(object):
2       def __init__(self, *args, **kwds):
3           [...]
4           self.runlist = ['surface_fluxes', 'bottom_fluxes',
5                           'density', 'advection',
6                           'vertical_mixing', 'tracers']
7           [...]
8       def execute_runlist(self):
9           for imethodname in self.runlist:
10              f = getattr(self, imethodname)
11              f()
12      def surface_fluxes(self):
13          [... calculate surface fluxes ...]
14      def bottom_fluxes(self):
15          [... calculate bottom boundary fluxes ...]
16      [...]
```

Most of this code are placeholders (denoted by the square bracketed ellipses), but the `execute_runlist` method definition (lines 9–11) is complete (barring error checking) and bears comment. That method iterates through the `runlist` attribute list of subroutine (i.e., method) names, uses each name to retrieve the method itself, then executes the method. The variable `f` in the code is *the actual method* given by a string in the `runlist` attribute; the `getattr` function will give you the item attached to an object, regardless of whether it is an attribute or method (thus, `getattr` is somewhat misnamed). In this sense, objects actually only have attributes; it's just some attributes are data while others are functions that act on data. Once `f` is assigned to a method, the syntax `f()` calls the function, just like any other function call. (As we saw in Section 6.5, functions are objects in Python like any other object, and they can be stored, assigned, etc. So the `f()` call is no different than if I had typed `self.surface_fluxes()`, `self.bottom_fluxes`, etc.)

There are a variety of possible ways to use flexibility in subroutine execution order; here's one. Sometimes, the execution order of climate model subroutines affects model results. Thus, you might want to do a series of runs where subroutine execution order is shuffled. To do this using traditionally procedural languages, you would have to create separate versions of the source code and manually change the order of subroutine calling in each version of the code (then recompile, run, etc.). Using the `Model` class above,

8.4. DYNAMICALLY CHANGING SUBROUTINE EXECUTION ORDER (OPTIONAL)

you would just create multiple instances of `Model` and create different versions of the `runlist` attribute where the order of the items in the list are shuffled.

How to do the list shuffling?[6] One way is to make use of the function `permutations` (from the itertools module) which will create an iterator that will step you through all permutations of the argument of `permutations`. Thus, this code:

Stepping through permutations.

```
a = itertools.permutations([0,1,2])
for i in a:
    print i
```

will print out all the different orderings of the list `[0,1,2]`:

```
(0, 1, 2)
(0, 2, 1)
(1, 0, 2)
(1, 2, 0)
(2, 0, 1)
(2, 1, 0)
```

(Tuples result, so we will remember to use the `list` conversion function to give ourselves a list.)

We can apply this permutation function to the `runlist` attribute; instead of permuting a list of numbers, we will permute a list of strings. Each permutation will be set to the `runlist` attribute of the `Model` instance and executed. The code to do this would (basically) be:

```
1  import itertools
2  mymodel = Model([... input arguments ...])
3  runlist_copy = list(mymodel.runlist)
4  permute = itertools.permutations(runlist_copy)
5  for irunlist in permute:
6      mymodel.runlist = list(irunlist)
7      mymodel.execute_runlist()
```

Again, what have we done? By using lists and other Python helper functions on a model encapsulated in a class, we've created a series of model

---

[6]For more on shuffling and permutations in Python, see http://stackoverflow.com/questions/104420/how-to-generate-all-permutations-of-a-list-in-python (accessed August 10, 2012).

8.4. DYNAMICALLY CHANGING SUBROUTINE EXECUTION ORDER (OPTIONAL)

runs each of which executes the model's subroutines using one of the possible permutations of subroutine execution order. The lines of code needed to make this series of model runs is trivial (just 7). OOP, plus Python's powerful data structures and amazing library of modules, enables AOS users to easily use atmosphere and ocean models in ways that traditional methods of programming make difficult (or even impossible).

An aside on assignment by reference vs. value: In line 3 above, I create a copy of the `runlist` attribute to make sure the `permutations` function is not acting on a list that will be changing in the loop. I do this because Python, for most variable types, including lists, does assignment by reference rather than value. Thus, the assignment in line 6 will propagate to all references to `mymodel.runlist`. By using the `list` function on `mymodel.runlist` in line 3, I make sure that `runlist_copy` is separate in memory from `mymodel.runlist`. Here's another example to make clearer the distinction between assignment by reference vs. value:

Python assignment is usually by reference rather than value.

Example 53 (Assignment by reference vs. value):

Assignment by reference means that the assignment creates a pointer or alias to the memory location given by another variable while assignment by value means that the assignment creates a copy of that other variable and points to that copy. Consider the following lines of code:

```
>>> a = [1,2,3]
>>> b = a
>>> b[1] = 6.5
```

where I create a list a, assign the variable b to a, and then replace the oneth element of b with another value. Because the assignment of variable b to a is done by reference, not value, my replacement of the oneth element of b *also changes* the corresponding element of a. A print of a and b will show this:

```
>>> print b
[1, 6.5, 3]
>>> print a
[1, 6.5, 3]
```

Copying using deepcopy.

In other words, the b = a assignment did not create a copy of a but creates a pointer to the memory location of a and assigns the name b to that pointer. If what you wanted was for b to be an actual copy of b, you can use the `deepcopy` function of the copy module. Thus, this code:

```
>>> import copy
>>> a = [1,2,3]
>>> b = copy.deepcopy(a)
>>> b[1] = 6.5
>>> print b
[1, 6.5, 3]
>>> print a
[1, 2, 3]
```

as you can see, assigns b to a copy of a so any changes in b are separate from a, and vice versa.

Most datatypes in Python assign by reference. Simple datatypes like integers, floats, strings, etc. assign by value. Thus, for an integer scalar:

```
>>> a = 3
>>> b = a
>>> a = 6
>>> print b
3
```

we see that a change in a does not propagate to the variable b. (By the way, if you want to find the memory location of an object, you can use the id function. Two objects that both point to the same memory location should have the same id value.)

As a final aside: The use of "runlists" is only one way that an object encapsulation of atmosphere and ocean models can make those models more usable and powerful. I wrote a paper in *Geosci. Model Dev.* (Lin, 2009) that described such an object encapsulation for an intermediate-level tropical atmospheric circulation model and also demonstrated a hybrid Python-Fortran implementation of an atmospheric model; see http://www.geosci-model-dev.net/2/1/2009/gmd-2-1-2009.html if you're interested.

8.5 Summary

There's no denying it: object-oriented programming (OOP) is hard to learn. Anecdotal reports suggest even professional programmers need to work on around three OOP projects before they become proficient in OOP (Curtis, 1995). The dynamic nature of objects, however, permits one to do analysis

8.5. SUMMARY

in ways that would be much harder to do using traditional procedural programming. In this chapter, we saw three such AOS examples: Simpler handling of missing values and metadata, dynamic variable management, and dynamic subroutine execution ordering. OOP is not just a way of reorganizing data and functions, but a way of making more kinds of analysis possible for scientists to do. While Python works fine as a procedural language—so you can write Python programs similar to the way you would write Fortran, IDL, Matlab, etc. programs—the object-oriented aspects of Python provide some of the greatest benefit for AOS users. It's a steep learning curve, but well worth it.

Chapter 9

Visualization: Basic Line and Contour Plots

With so much of the analysis of AOS problems requiring graphing or visualization of some sort, no scientist's toolkit is complete without a robust visualization suite. Because Python is an open-source programming language, you have not just one visualization suite but several to choose from. For AOS graphics, NCAR's PyNGL, UV-CDAT's Visualization Control System (vcs), and matplotlib are three powerful packages that can handle most AOS visualization tasks. While each has its own strengths and weaknesses, in this chapter we will focus on matplotlib and its 2-D graphics routines to create line and contour plots.[1]

(By the way, just a heads-up that in this chapter, the plots and tables will usually be in figures that float to wherever on the page works best for optimizing the page. Plots and tables may not immediately follow where they are first mentioned.)

9.1 What is matplotlib?

Matplotlib, as its name suggests, emulates the Matlab plotting suite: commands look like Matlab commands. It has a function-centric interface adequate for the needs of most users (especially first-time users), but the entire suite is object-based, so power users have fine-grained control over the de-

---

[1] PyNGL implements the graphing resources of the NCAR Command Language (NCL) into Python (NCL has more "high-level" functions, but PyNGL can draw everything NCL can). Vcs is the original plotting module for CDAT and UV-CDAT. Its default settings are not always pretty, but they make use of the masks and metadata attached to masked variables, so plotting is fast. Section 10.2 tells you where to go to obtain these packages.

tails of their plots. (In this chapter, I won't talk much about the object-based interface.) Matplotlib's default plots also look uncommonly beautiful, which was the intention of the package's primary author, John Hunter. Finally, matplotlib has a broad user community from many disciplines, so a lot of people contribute to it and templates/examples exist for many different kinds of plots.

The submodule pyplot defines the functional interface for matplotlib. Pyplot is often imported by:

```
import matplotlib.pyplot as plt
```

Unless otherwise stated, you may assume in the examples in this chapter that the above import has been done prior to any matplotlib calls being run.

Do the online pyplot tutorial. It's very good! The online pyplot tutorial is very good. In this chapter, we'll cover only a few of the topics found in there; I encourage you to go through it all on your own: http://matplotlib.sourceforge.net/users/pyplot_tutorial.html. The online gallery of examples is also very illuminating: http://matplotlib.sourceforge.net/gallery.html.

9.2 Basic line plots

Plot makes plots and show visualizes them. Line plots are created by the pyplot `plot` function. Once created, matplotlib keeps track of what plot is the "current" plot. Subsequent commands (e.g., to make a label) are applied to the current plot.

The `show` function visualizes (i.e., displays) the plot to screen. If you have more than one figure, call `show` after all plots are defined to visualize all the plots at once. Consider the following example:

Example 54 (Your first line plot):

Type in this example into a file and run it in the Python interpreter:

```
import matplotlib.pyplot as plt
plt.plot([1, 2, 3, 4], [1, 2.1, 1.8, 4.3])
plt.axis([0, 8, -2, 7])
plt.xlabel('Automatic Range')
plt.ylabel('Made-up Numbers')
plt.show()
```

What did you get? Based on what's output, what do you think each of the commands do?

9.2. BASIC LINE PLOTS

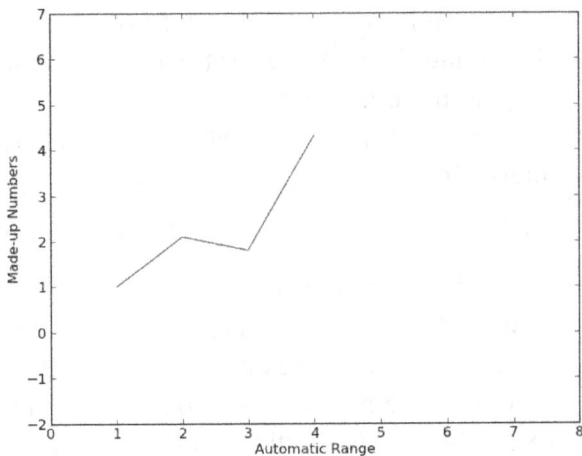

Figure 9.1: Graph created by the code in Example 54.

Solution and discussion: You should have obtained a plot like the one shown in Figure 9.1.

Line 2 of the code creates the plot, and the two list input arguments provide the *x*- and *y*-values, respectively. (I could have used NumPy arrays instead of lists as inputs.) The `axis` function in line 3 gives the range for the *x*- and *y*-axes, with the first two elements of the input parameter list giving the lower and upper bounds of the *x*-axis and the last two elements giving the lower and upper bounds of the *y*-axis. Lines 4 and 5 label the *x*- and *y*-axes, respectively, and the `show` function displays the graph on the screen.

9.2.1 Controlling line and marker formatting

To control line and marker features, you can use the appropriate keyword input parameters with the `plot` function, e.g.:

Controlling linestyle, markers, etc.

```
plt.plot([1, 2, 3, 4], [1, 2.1, 1.8, 4.3],
         linestyle='--', linewidth=5.0,
         marker='*', markersize=20.0,
         markeredgewidth=2.0,
         markerfacecolor='w')
```

9.2. BASIC LINE PLOTS

Note how `linestyle`, `marker`, and `markerfacecolor` use special string codes to specify the line and marker type and formatting. The `plot` call above uses a dashed line and a white star for the marker. Linewidth, marker size, and marker edge width are in points.

Instead of using keyword input parameters, you can also specify line color and type and marker color and type as a string third argument, e.g.:

```
plt.plot([1, 2, 3, 4], [1, 2.1, 1.8, 4.3], 'r*--')
```

Notice that this third argument contains *all* the codes to specify line color, line type, marker color, and marker type. That is to say, all these codes can be specified in one string. In the above example, the color of the marker and connecting line is set to red, the marker is set to star, and the linestyle is set to dashed. (The marker edge color is still the default, black, however.)

Line and marker property listings. Tables 9.1 and 9.2 list some of the basic linestyles and marker codes. For a more complete list of linestyles, marker codes, and basically all the line and marker properties that can possibly be set, see the following web pages:

- Linestyles: http://matplotlib.sourceforge.net/api/artist_api.html#matplotlib.lines.Line2D.set_linestyle

- Marker symbol types: http://matplotlib.sourceforge.net/api/artist_api.html#matplotlib.lines.Line2D.set_marker.

- Line and marker properties: http://matplotlib.sourceforge.net/api/artist_api.html#matplotlib.lines.Line2D.

Table 9.3 lists some of the color codes available in pyplot.

9.2.2 Annotation and adjusting the font size of labels

Annotation and font size. We introduced the `xlabel` and `ylabel` functions in Example 54 to annotate the *x*- and *y*-axes, respectively. To place a title at the top of the plot, use the `title` function, whose basic syntax is the same as `xlabel` and `ylabel`. General annotation uses the `text` function, whose syntax is:

```
plt.text(<x-location>, <y-location>, <string to write>)
```

The *x*- and *y*-locations are, by default, in terms of **data coordinates.** For all four functions (`xlabel`, `ylabel`, `title`, and `text`), font size is controlled by the `size` keyword input parameter. When set to a floating point value, `size` specifies the size of the text in points.

Using LaTeX to annotate plots. Here's one cool feature: matplotlib gives you the ability to use LaTeX to render text! See http://matplotlib.sourceforge.net/users/usetex.html for details.

9.2. BASIC LINE PLOTS

Linestyle	String Code
Solid line	-
Single dashed line	--
Single dashed-dot line	-.
Dotted line	:

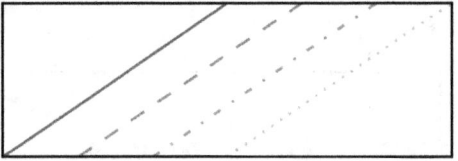

```
1   import numpy as N
2   import matplotlib.pyplot as plt
3   plt.figure(1, figsize=(3,1))
4   plt.plot( N.arange(4),   N.arange(4), '-', \
5            N.arange(4)+1, N.arange(4), '--', \
6            N.arange(4)+2, N.arange(4), '-.', \
7            N.arange(4)+3, N.arange(4), ':' )
8   plt.gca().axes.get_xaxis().set_visible(False)
9   plt.gca().axes.get_yaxis().set_visible(False)
10  plt.savefig('pyplot_linestyles.png', dpi=300)
```

Table 9.1: Some linestyle codes in pyplot, a high-resolution line plot showing the lines generated by the linestyle codes, and the code to generate the plot. Lines 8–9 turn-off the *x*- and *y*-axis tick marks and labels (see "matplotlib.pyplot.gca," http://matplotlib.sourceforge.net/api/pyplot_api.html and http://stackoverflow.com/a/2176591, both accessed August 13, 2012). A full explanation of these lines is beyond the scope of this book; please see the sources for more information. Note **show** is not called since I only want a file version of the plot.

9.2. BASIC LINE PLOTS

Marker	String Code
Circle	o
Diamond	D
Point	.
Plus	+
Square	s
Star	*
Up Triangle	^
X	x

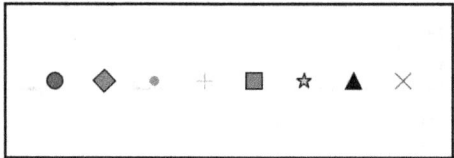

```
1   import numpy as N
2   import matplotlib.pyplot as plt
3   plt.figure(1, figsize=(3,1))
4   plt.plot( 1, 1, 'o', \
5            2, 1, 'D', \
6            3, 1, '.', \
7            4, 1, '+', \
8            5, 1, 's', \
9            6, 1, '*', \
10           7, 1, '^', \
11           8, 1, 'x' )
12  plt.axis([0, 9, 0, 2])
13  plt.gca().axes.get_xaxis().set_visible(False)
14  plt.gca().axes.get_yaxis().set_visible(False)
15  plt.savefig('pyplot_markers.png', dpi=300)
```

Table 9.2: Some marker codes in pyplot, a high-resolution line plot showing the markers generated by the marker codes, and the code to generate the plot. Lines 12–13 turn-off the *x*- and *y*-axis tick marks and labels. See Table 9.1 for sources and more information.

Color	String Code
Black	k
Blue	b
Green	g
Red	r
White	w

Table 9.3: Some color codes in pyplot. See http://matplotlib.sourceforge.net/api/colors_api.html for a full list of the built-in colors codes as well as for ways to access other colors.

9.2. BASIC LINE PLOTS

Example 55 (Annotation and font size):
Consider this code:

```
plt.plot([1, 2, 3, 4], [1, 2.1, 1.8, 4.3])
plt.xlabel('Automatic Range')
plt.ylabel('Made-up Numbers')
plt.title('Zeroth Plot', size=36.0)
plt.text(2.5, 2.0, 'My cool label', size=18.0)
plt.show()
```

What does this code do?

Solution and discussion: The above code produces a graph like the one in Figure 9.2. (Note that I resized that graph to fit it nicely on the page, so the text sizes as shown may not be equal to the values given in `size`.)

9.2.3 Plotting multiple figures and curves

Multiple independent figures.
If you have have multiple independent figures (not multiple curves on one plot), call the `figure` function before you call `plot` to label the figure accordingly. A subsequent call to that figure's number makes that figure current. For instance:

Example 56 (Line plots of multiple independent figures):
Consider this code:

```
1  plt.figure(3)
2  plt.plot([5, 6, 7, 8], [1, 1.8, -0.4, 4.3],
3          marker='o')
4  plt.figure(4)
5  plt.plot([0.1, 0.2, 0.3, 0.4], [8, -2, 5.3, 4.2],
6          linestyle='-.')
7  plt.figure(3)
8  plt.title('First Plot')
```

What does this code do?

9.2. BASIC LINE PLOTS

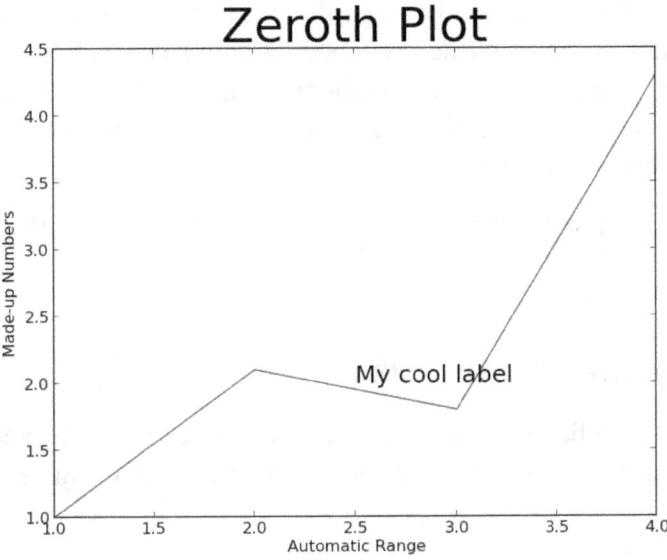

Figure 9.2: Graph created by the code in Example 55.

Solution and discussion: Line 1 creates a figure and gives it the name "3". Lines 2–3 (which is a single logical line to the interpreter) makes a line plot with a circle as the marker to the figure named "3". Line 4 creates a figure named "4", and lines 5–6 make a line plot with a dash-dot linestyle to that figure. Line 7 makes figure "3" the current plot again, and the final line adds a title to figure "3".

To plot multiple curves on a single plot, you can string the set of three arguments (*x*-locations, *y*-locations, and line/marker properties) for each plot one right after the other. For instance:

Multiple curves on one plot.

Example 57 (Line plot of multiple curves on one figure):
Consider this code:

```
plt.plot([0, 1, 2, 3], [1, 2, 3, 4], '--o',
         [1, 3, 5, 9], [8, -2, 5.3, 4.2], '-D')
```

What does it do?

9.2. BASIC LINE PLOTS

Solution and discussion: The first three arguments specify the *x*- and *y*-locations of the first curve, which will be plot using a dashed line and a circle as the marker. The second three arguments specify the *x*- and *y*-locations of the second curve, which will be plot with a solid line and a diamond as the marker. Both curves will be on the same figure.

9.2.4 Adjusting the plot size

Adjusting plot size.

One easy way of adjusting the plot size is to set the `figsize` and `dpi` keyword input parameters in the `figure` command.[2] For instance, this call to `figure`:

```
plt.figure(1, figsize=(3,1), dpi=300)
```

before the call to the `plot` command, will make figure "1" three inches wide and one inch high, with a resolution of 300 dots per inch (dpi). The plot associated with Table 9.1 shows a code and plot example that explicitly specifies the `figsize` keyword.

9.2.5 Saving figures to a file

Save figure.

To write the plot out to a file, you can use the `savefig` function. For example, to write out the current figure to a PNG file called *testplot.png*, at 300 dpi, type:

```
plt.savefig('testplot.png', dpi=300)
```

Resolution and figure size in figure vs. savefig.

Here we specify an output resolution using the optional `dpi` keyword parameter; if left out, the matplotlib default resolution will be used. Note that it is not enough for you to set `dpi` in your `figure` command to get an output file at a specific resolution. The `dpi` setting in `figure` will control what resolution `show` displays at while the `dpi` setting in `savefig` will control the output file's resolution; however, the `figsize` parameter in `figure` controls the figure size for both `show` and `savefig`.

You can also save figures to a file using the GUI save button that is part of the plot window displayed on the screen when you execute the `show` function. If you save the plot using the save button, it will save at the default

---

[2]http://stackoverflow.com/a/638443 (accessed August 13, 2012).

resolution, even if you specify a different resolution in your `figure` command; use `savefig` if you want to write out your file at a specific resolution.

Most of the code for the examples in this section (9.2) are found in the file *example-viz-line.py* in *course_files/code_files*.

9.3 Exercise on basic line plots

▷ **Exercise 27 (Line plot of a surface air temperature timeseries):**
Read in the monthly mean surface/near-surface air temperature and the time axis from the provided NCEP/NCAR Reanalysis 1 netCDF dataset. (The example data is in *course_files/datasets* in the file *air.mon.mean.nc*.) Extract a timeseries at one location (any location) on the Earth and plot the first 100 data points of air temperature vs. time. Annotate appropriately. Write the plot out to a PNG file.

Solution and discussion: Here's my solution. The plotting section using matplotlib starts with line 11:

```
1  import Scientific.IO.NetCDF as S
2  import matplotlib.pyplot as plt
3
4  fileobj = S.NetCDFFile('air.mon.mean.nc', mode='r')
5  T_arctic = fileobj.variables['air'].getValue()[0:100,0,0]
6  T_units = fileobj.variables['air'].units
7  time = fileobj.variables['time'].getValue()[0:100]
8  time_units = fileobj.variables['time'].units
9  fileobj.close()
10
11 plt.plot(time, T_arctic)
12 plt.xlabel('Time [' + time_units + ']')
13 plt.ylabel('Temperature [' + T_units + ']')
14
15 plt.savefig('exercise-T-line.png')
16 plt.show()
```

This code makes a plot like the one in Figure 9.3. Note how string concatenation, coupled with each variable's `units` metadata values in the netCDF file, make it easy to annotate the plot with the units.

On some installations, if you call `show` before `savefig`, things do not always write correctly to the file, so in my code I call `savefig` first, just *Call savefig before show.*

9.4. BASIC CONTOUR PLOTS

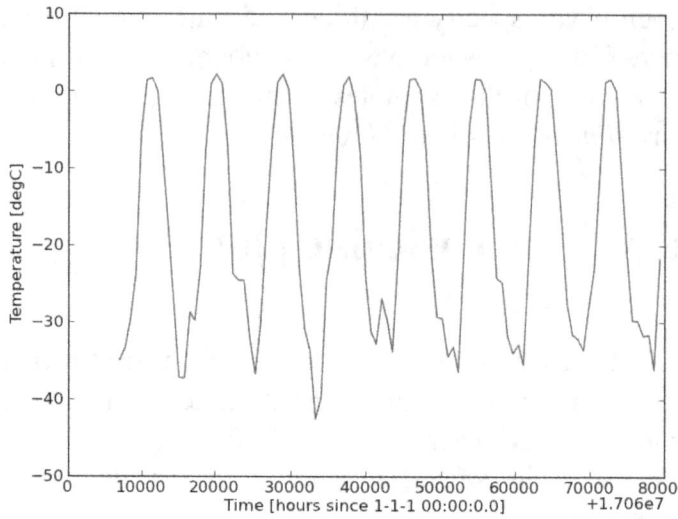

Figure 9.3: Graph created by the solution code to Exercise 27.

to be safe. Of course, if you only want the plot as a file, just use `savefig` without calling `show`.

This code is in the file *exercise-viz-line.py* in the *course_files/code_files* subdirectory.

9.4 Basic contour plots

A number of the aspects of plotting (e.g., saving a figure to a file, etc.) work for contour plots exactly the same as for line plots. In this section, we won't rehash those common aspects.

Contour plots using contour.
Contour plots are created by matplotlib's `contour` function. A basic contour plot is generated by:

```
plt.contour(X, Y, Z, nlevels)
```

where Z is a 2-D array of the values to contour with and X and Y are the *x*- and *y*-locations, respectively, of the Z values (X and Y can be 2-D arrays or 1-D vectors, the latter if the grid is regular). The optional `nlevels` parameter tells how many automatically generated contour levels to make.

The nlevels parameter.
The `levels` keyword controls exactly which levels to draw contours at, e.g.:

```
plt.contour(X, Y, Z, levels=[-2, -1, 0, 1, 2])
```

9.4. BASIC CONTOUR PLOTS

To make dashed negative contours, set the `colors` keyword to `'k'`:

```
plt.contour(X, Y, Z, colors='k')
```

Making negative contours dashed.

This setting makes the all the contours black. Matplotlib then renders the negative contours using the value of an "rc setting" that defaults to dashed.[3]

While you can do nice default contour maps just by calling the `contour` function, a number of contour map functions take a contour map object as input. Thus, it's better to save the map to a variable:

```
mymap = plt.contour(X, Y, Z)
```

Saving the contour map to a variable so you can pass it into other formatting functions.

Then, to add contour labels, for instance, use the `clabel` function (this is a function that asks for a contour map object as input):

```
mymap = plt.contour(X, Y, Z)
plt.clabel(mymap, fontsize=12)
```

The optional keyword `fontsize` sets the font size (in points).

For filled contours, use the `contourf` function. The color maps available for filled contour maps are attributes of the `pyplot` module attribute `cm`. You specify which color map to use via the `cmap` keyword:

Making filled contour maps.

```
mymap = plt.contourf(X, Y, Z, cmap=plt.cm.RdBu)
```

A list of predefined color maps is located at http://www.scipy.org/Cookbook/Matplotlib/Show_colormaps. To add a color bar that shows the scale of the plot, make a call to `colorbar` that uses the filled contour plot object as input:

List of predefined color maps and adding color bars.

```
plt.colorbar(mymap, orientation='horizontal',
             levels=[-2, -1, 0, 1, 2])
```

The `orientation` keyword specifies the orientation of the color bar, as you'd expect ☺. The `levels` keyword is set to a list that specifies what levels to label on the color bar.

To make a contour map that's both lined and filled, make a filled contour map call then a line contour map call (or vice versa), e.g.:

---

[3]The rc setting is `contour.negative_linestyle` and can be changed in the *matplotlibrc* file. See http://matplotlib.sourceforge.net/users/customizing.html for details (accessed August 17, 2012).

9.5. EXERCISE ON BASIC CONTOUR PLOTS

```
plt.contourf(lonall, latall, T_time0, 10,
             cmap=plt.cm.Reds)
plt.contour(lonall, latall, T_time0, 10,
            colors='k')
```

Both contour maps will be placed on the same figure.

Making wind barbs.
Lastly, atmospheric scientists are often interested in wind barbs: these are generated with the `barbs` method of objects generated by the matplotlib `subplot` function. See http://matplotlib.sourceforge.net/examples/pylab_examples/barb_demo.html for an example.

Before Q&A   After Q&A

9.5 Exercise on basic contour plots

▷ **Exercise 28 (Contour plot of surface air temperature):**
Read in the monthly mean surface/near-surface air temperature from the NCEP/NCAR Reanalysis 1 netCDF dataset provided. Also read in the latitude and longitude vectors from the dataset. Extract a single timeslice of the temperature and plot a contour map. Annotate appropriately. Write the plot out to a PNG file. Hint: The NumPy function `meshgrid` can be your friend (see Example 32), though it may not be necessary.

9.5. EXERCISE ON BASIC CONTOUR PLOTS

Solution and discussion: Here's my solution:

```
1   import numpy as N
2   import Scientific.IO.NetCDF as S
3   import matplotlib.pyplot as plt
4
5   fileobj = S.NetCDFFile('air.mon.mean.nc', mode='r')
6   T_time0 = fileobj.variables['air'].getValue()[0,:,:]
7   T_units = fileobj.variables['air'].units
8   lon = fileobj.variables['lon'].getValue()
9   lon_units = fileobj.variables['lon'].units
10  lat = fileobj.variables['lat'].getValue()
11  lat_units = fileobj.variables['lat'].units
12  fileobj.close()
13
14  [lonall, latall] = N.meshgrid(lon, lat)
15
16  mymapf = plt.contourf(lonall, latall, T_time0, 10,
17                        cmap=plt.cm.Reds)
18  mymap = plt.contour(lonall, latall, T_time0, 10,
19                      colors='k')
20  plt.clabel(mymap, fontsize=12)
21  plt.axis([0, 360, -90, 90])
22  plt.xlabel('Longitude [' + lon_units + ']')
23  plt.ylabel('Latitude [' + lat_units + ']')
24  plt.colorbar(mymapf, orientation='horizontal')
25
26  plt.savefig('exercise-T-contour.png')
27  plt.show()
```

Lines 5–12 read in the data from the netCDF file. In line 6, we obtain the 2-D slab of surface air temperature at time zero and assign it to the array variable `T_time0`. The `lon` and `lat` variables, created in lines 8 and 10, are 1-D vectors. To be on the safe side, we want 2-D versions of these vectors, which we create in line 14 using `meshgrid` and assign as `lonall` and `latall`. Line 16 specifies that we plot the contour plot with 10 contour intervals, and in line 17, we specify a red gradient color map to use for the contour interval filling.

In lines 18–19, we create a contour map of lines only, to superimpose on top of the filled contour plot. We assign the result of the `contour` call to `mymap`, which we'll use with the `clabel` function in line 20 (that generates

9.6. SUPERIMPOSING A MAP

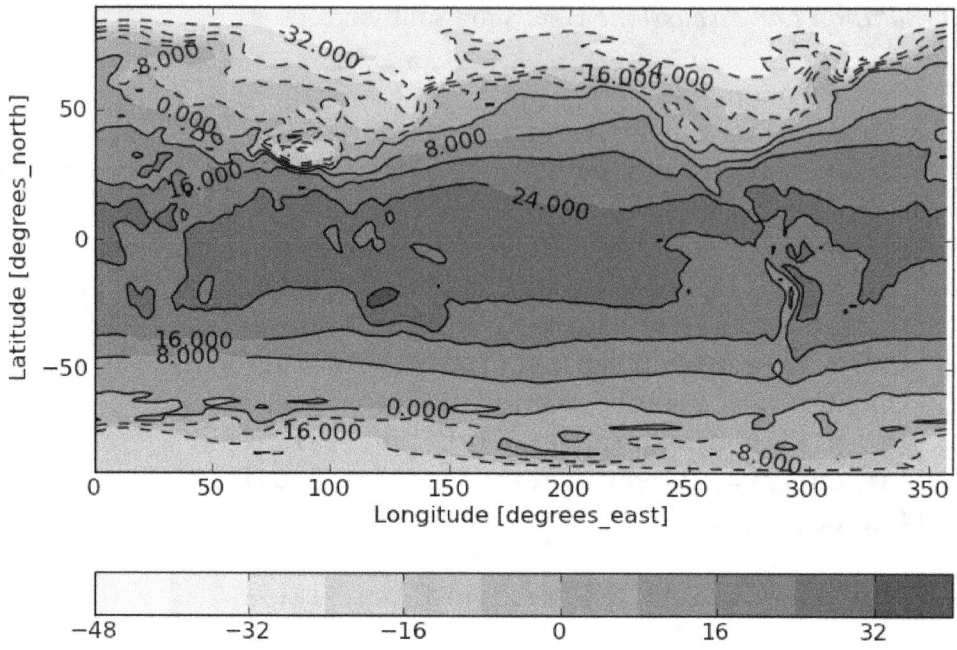

Figure 9.4: Graph created by the solution code to Exercise 28.

the contour labels). Line 21 specifies the axes range using the `axis` function, labeling occurs in lines 22–23, the color map in line 24, and the last two lines save the figure to a file and display the figure on the screen.

Note how the results of both the `contourf` and `contour` calls need to be assigned to objects which are used by the `colorbar` and `clabel` functions as input (in lines 24 and 20, respectively). Also note that on some installations, if you call `show` before `savefig`, things do not always write correctly to the file, so in my code I call `savefig` first, just to be safe.

The code generates a plot like the one in Figure 9.4. This code is in the file *exercise-viz-contour.py* in the *code_files* subdirectory of the *course_files* directory.

9.6 Superimposing a map

The Basemap package and map projections. Often, AOS users will want to superimpose a map of some sort (e.g., continental outlines) onto a contour plot. To do so, you need to use the Basemap package, which handles map projection setup for matplotlib. Note, however, that Basemap is a separate package from matplotlib, is distributed under a different license, and often has to be installed separately.[4] For many operating system environments, you need to build Basemap from source. (It is, however, a Debian package in Ubuntu 12.04.)[5] If you have the full version of the Enthought Python Distribution (EPD), Basemap is installed for you; Basemap, however, is not part of EPD Free.

To create a map and then superimpose a contour plot on the map, follow these steps:

Steps to creating a contour plot on a map.

- Instantiate an instance of the `Basemap` class.

- Use methods of that instance to draw continents, etc.

- Map the 2-D latitude and longitude coordinates of your dataset to the coordinates in the map projection by calling your `Basemap` instance with the dataset coordinates as input arguments.

- Make your contour plot using regular matplotlib commands.

This will become much clearer with an example:

Example 58 (Contour plot on a cylindrical projection map limited to the global Tropics):

Assume you have three 2-D arrays as input: `data`, which is the data being contoured, and `lonall` and `latall`, which give the longitudes and latitudes (in degrees), respectively, of the elements of `data`. The code to create the contour plot and the map is:

```
import numpy as N
import matplotlib.pyplot as plt
import mpl_toolkits.basemap as bm
mapproj = bm.Basemap(projection='cyl',
                     llcrnrlat=-20.0, llcrnrlon=-180.0,
                     urcrnrlat=20.0, urcrnrlon=180.0)
mapproj.drawcoastlines()
mapproj.drawparallels(N.array([-20, -10, 0, 10, 20]),
                      labels=[1,0,0,0])
mapproj.drawmeridians(N.array([-180, -90, 0, 90, 180]),
                      labels=[0,0,0,1])
lonproj, latproj = mapproj(lonall, latall)
plt.contour(lonproj, latproj, data)
```

---

[4]See http://sourceforge.net/projects/matplotlib/files/matplotlib-toolkits for the downloads (accessed August 16, 2012).

[5]See http://packages.ubuntu.com/en/precise/python-mpltoolkits.basemap for a description of the package (accessed August 16, 2012).

9.6. SUPERIMPOSING A MAP

In lines 4–6, what do you think the keywords do? The `labels` keywords in lines 9 and 11?

Solution and discussion: The first three lines of the code imports the needed packages. Notice that Basemap is normally found as a subpackage of the mpl_toolkits package. Lines 4–6 create `mapproj`, a Basemap instance. The keyword input parameters set the projection (cylindrical) and give the "corner" latitude and longitude values of the map: `llcrnrlat` is the lower-left corner's latitude, `urcrnrlon` is the upper-right corner's longitude, etc.

<small>Basemap map projection parameters.</small>

Once the `mapproj` Basemap instance is created, we use methods attached to the instance to draw coastlines (line 7), latitude lines (lines 8–9), and longitude lines (lines 10–11). The positional input argument for `drawparallels` and `drawmeridians` specifies the locations at which to draw the latitude and longitude lines. The `labels` keyword is set to a 4-element list of integers that specify where to draw the labels. If the first element is set to 1, labels are drawn to the left of the plot, if the second element is set to 1, labels are drawn to the right of the plot, and the third and fourth elements control the top and bottom labels, respectively. Thus, line 9 specifies latitude line labels on the left side of the plot (only) and line 11 specifies longitude line labels at the bottom of the plot (only).

<small>Basemap instance methods create coastlines, etc.</small>

Line 12 calls the `mapproj` instance as if it were a function. The 2-D longitude and latitude arrays are passed into the call. Two 2-D arrays are returned that specify the longitude and latitude values, but altered to account for the projection, that can then be passed into a contour plot call, along with the data to contour, as is done in line 13.

We haven't really talked about calling object instances, but indeed, we can define a special method `__call__` in a class that will be executed when you call an instance (that is, treat the instance like it were a function). That's essentially what is happening in line 12. Note that calling an instance is not the same as **instantiating** the instance!

<small>Calling object instances.</small>

Basemap supports many different types of projections, and the input parameters when instantiating a `Basemap` object will change depending on the projection you specify. The SciPy Cookbook entry for Basemap gives a nice introduction: http://www.scipy.org/Cookbook/Matplotlib/Maps. Also see the Basemap documentation: http://matplotlib.github.com/basemap.

9.7 Exercise on superimposing a map

▷ **Exercise 29 (Contour plot of surface air temperature with continental outlines):**

Redo Exercise 28 but superimpose a map with continental outlines on it.

Solution and discussion: To save space, I only provide the core of my solution here. The full code is in the file *exercise-viz-basemap.py* in the *code_files* subdirectory of the *course_files* directory:

```
mapproj = bm.Basemap(projection='cyl',
                     llcrnrlat=-90.0, llcrnrlon=0.0,
                     urcrnrlat=90.0, urcrnrlon=360.0)
mapproj.drawcoastlines()
mapproj.drawparallels(N.array([-90, -45, 0, 45, 90]),
                      labels=[1,0,0,0])
mapproj.drawmeridians(N.array([0, 90, 180, 270, 360]),
                      labels=[0,0,0,1])
lonall, latall = mapproj(lon2d, lat2d)

mymapf = plt.contourf(lonall, latall, T_time0, 10,
                      cmap=plt.cm.Reds)
mymap = plt.contour(lonall, latall, T_time0, 10,
                    colors='k')
plt.clabel(mymap, fontsize=12)
plt.title('Air Temperature [' + T_units + ']')
plt.colorbar(mymapf, orientation='horizontal')

plt.savefig('exercise-T-basemap.png')
plt.show()
```

This code makes a plot like the one in Figure 9.5.

This code is essentially a combination of Exercise 28 and Example 58. The one difference is in lines 2–3 of this exercise, where I specify the longitude corner keywords by the range 0 to 360 degrees instead of −180 to 180 degrees (as in Example 58). Since the data starts with 0 degrees longitude, I decided to put that in the lower-left corner. But referencing longitude by negative longitude values works fine in Basemap.

9.8. SUMMARY

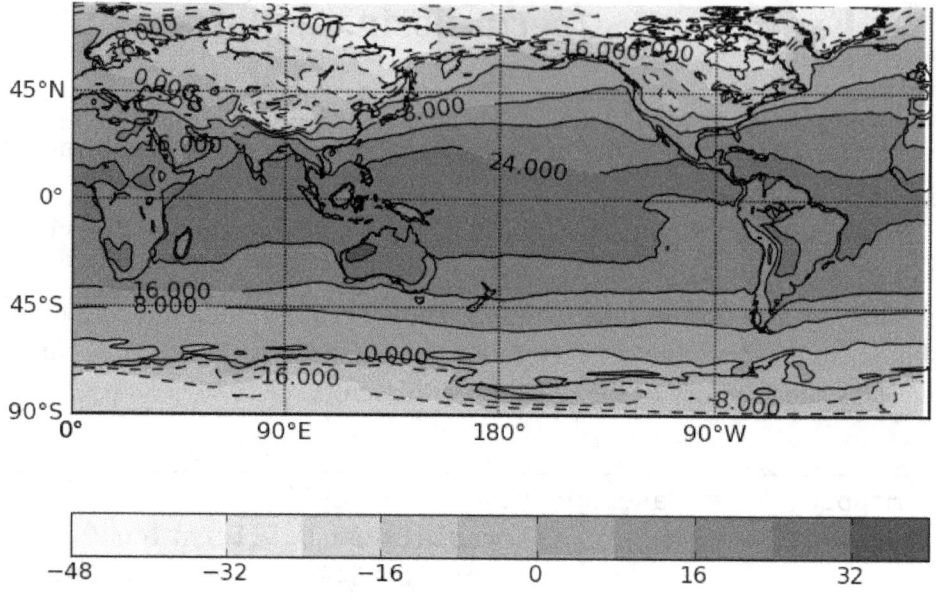

Figure 9.5: Graph created by the solution code to Exercise 29.

9.8 Summary

Basic Python visualization using matplotlib is very much like what you're probably used to using in Matlab and IDL. Coupled with the Basemap module, matplotlib enables you to do the basic line and contour plots that form the bread-and-butter of AOS visualization. Details on matplotlib are found at http://matplotlib.sourceforge.net.

<small>Other Python AOS visualization packages.</small> This chapter, of course, only scratches the surface regarding Python visualization. The PyAOS website keeps a list of packages that may be of interest to AOS users (http://pyaos.johnny-lin.com/?page_id=117). Some packages of note include:

- ParaView: Analysis and visualization package for very large datasets.

- PyGrADS: Python interface to GrADS.

- PyNGL: All of the basic functionality of NCAR Graphics in a Python interface.

- UV-CDAT: Ultrascale Visualization-Climate Data Analysis Tools.

- VisTrails: Visualization tool with workflow management that tracks the provenance of the visualization and data.

- VPython: An easy-to-use 3-D visualization and animation environment.

Unlike proprietary languages which have only one visualization engine integrated with the language, Python's open-source nature permits radical experimentation with different methods of implementing visualization tools. This does create some confusion, and can make installation a bear, but it also provides you the right visualization tool for your specific needs. Have a very large dataset? Try ParaView. Is workflow provenance integration vital to you? Give VisTrails and UV-CDAT a shot. Want to do really simple 3-D animation for educational modeling? VPython is a snap. But for many everyday visualization tasks, matplotlib works fine.

9.8. SUMMARY

Chapter 10

What Next?

Congratulations! You've taken the first step into an amazing and exciting new world. Python, with its modern computer science methods, enormous diversity of packages, and clear syntax, will enable you to write programs you never would have dreamed of before, to investigate science questions that would have been nearly impossible to address using traditional tools. As we wrap up this book and course, your intrepid tour guide of the Python world bids you a fond farewell, but not before suggesting some Python topics to address next, point out some Python packages that will be of interest to AOS users, and provide a list of references that you will find helpful as you continue to build-up your Python chops.

10.1 What Python topics would be good to cover next?

As you've gone through the book, you probably have come up with a personal list of topics you'd like to do more study on. Here is my list of topics for you to study next. See the references listed in Section 10.3 for more on most of these topics.

More NumPy routines and SciPy: We've only touched the surface of the calculations you can make with NumPy, and the SciPy package (imported by the `import scipy` command) offers even more mathematical and scientific packages.

Exception handling: We introduced exception handling in Section 3.16, but the real power and flexibility of exception handling is unleashed when you create your own special exception classes. This requires using inheritance (a topic outside the scope of this book), but enables you to test for and gracefully handle error conditions specific to your application.

10.1. WHAT PYTHON TOPICS WOULD BE GOOD TO COVER NEXT?

Documentation: We briefly discussed the most basic Python element to code documentation (aside from comment lines), the docstring, on p. 62. Besides docstrings, however, a number of packages exist to generate user guides, manuals, and API documentation. Two I like are Epydoc (http://epydoc.sourceforge.net) and Sphinx (http://sphinx.pocoo.org).

Unit testing: Many of the programs AOS users write are quick-and-dirty programs written by one individual with little to no documentation and testing. Unfortunately, as decades of software engineering experience has shown, this results in fragile, buggy code, and a lot of reinventing the wheel. Software testing is a *proven* way of increasing code quality and reliability (e.g., Basili and Selby, 1987). Python makes it easy for us to write unit tests, i.e., tests of small portions of code, through the unittest and pytest packages. The unittest package comes standard with every Python installation; pytest is available at http://pytest.org.

Platform-independent operating system commands: Python has been ported to nearly every operating system imaginable and through it offers the possibility of "write once, run anywhere" code. The os module (imported by `import os`) enables such platform independence by wrapping operating system commands in a Python interface. A submodule of os called path enables platform-independent handling of directory paths (it is imported by the `import os.path` command).

Environment customization: The sys module gives you access to variables that interact with the Python interpreter, such as the search path for Python modules (which, if you import sys by `import sys` is stored in the module attribute `sys.path`).

Wrapping Fortran routines: As cool as Python is, there is no way we can do our work without Fortran. There are too many lines of legacy code, and sometimes we need the speed of compiled code. Wouldn't it be nice if we could use Fortran routines from within Python? With f2py, this is not only possible but easy-peasy! And, if you have NumPy installed, you already have f2py. See http://www.scipy.org/F2py for more information.

Class inheritance: I mentioned this above when talking about exception handling, but this OOP concept has much more applicability than just in dealing with exceptions. Inheritance enables you to even more easily push functionality to the lowest appropriate level.

Advanced visualization: As I said in the end of Ch. 9, Python does not have only one visualization package but many, each with their own domains of competence. Check out PyNGL, vcs, VPython, etc.

10.2 Some packages of interest to AOS users

There is no possible way for me to list all the packages available for Python (as of August 2012, PyPI listed over 23,000 packages),[1] nor even all the packages of possible interest to AOS users. Here I mention just a few, organized by tasks AOS users conduct.

Data analysis: UV-CDAT is a veritable Swiss Army knife for climate data analysis. It includes specialized routines to deal with dates and times, spatial domains and regridding, climate model history files, OpenDAP, visualization, etc.; see http://uv-cdat.llnl.gov. UV-CDAT is an outgrowth of an older application CDAT; the CDAT pages have more documentation and are at http://www2-pcmdi.llnl.gov/cdat. (A lighter version that only has the core CDAT packages, Cdat-lite, is also available: see http://proj.badc.rl.ac.uk/cedaservices/wiki/CdatLite.) Finally, pandas is an interface on top of NumPy that enables you to reference subarrays using string labels (like dictionaries) and easily deal with missing values: see http://pandas.pydata.org.

PyGrADS provides a Python interface to the gridded data analysis and visualization system GrADS (http://opengrads.org/wiki/index.php?title=Python_Interface_to_GrADS).[2] PyNIO provides Python bindings to file i/o routines for formats of interest to AOS users; see http://www.pyngl.ucar.edu.

Visualization: PyNGL provides Python bindings to the NCAR Graphics Language; see http://www.pyngl.ucar.edu. PyGrADS, mentioned earlier, also helps AOS users visualize their data.

Mathematical and scientific functions: As I mentioned in Section 10.1, SciPy provides numerous mathematical and scientific routines (http://www.scipy.org). SAGE is another set of mathematical and scientific libraries (http://www.sagemath.org). Finally, RPy gives a Python interface to the powerful statistical language R (http://rpy.sourceforge.net).

GIS: ArcGIS scripting can be done in Python; see http://www.esri.com/software/arcgis. Other packages using Python that enable GIS manipulation include: PyKML (http://pypi.python.org/pypi/pykml), OpenClimateGIS (https://github.com/tylere/OpenClimateGIS), and GDAL (http://trac.osgeo.org/gdal/wiki/GdalOgrInPython).

Webservices: Python has a number of packages that enable you to do webservices. One of the most comprehensive is the Twisted package (http://twistedmatrix.com/trac). CherryPy is another, more accessible, package (http://cherrypy.org).

---

[1] http://pypi.python.org/pypi (accessed August 17, 2012).
[2] PyGrADS is part of the OpenGrADS project.

The PyAOS website maintains a list of packages of interest to AOS users. See: http://pyaos.johnny-lin.com/?page_id=20.

10.3 Additional references

Throughout the book, especially in this chapter, I've referenced a variety of resources, most of them online. In this section, I list places to look for more general help in using Python or resources that address specific topics that don't fit anywhere else. The Bibliography gives the full citation for books mentioned in this section.

Transitioning from Matlab/IDL to Python: Thankfully, you can find a number of equivalence sheets online for Matlab to Python and IDL to Python.[3] Of course, the languages aren't one-to-one identical to Python, but these sheets can still help with the transition.

Tutorials: There are a bunch of great Python tutorials, both online as well as in print. Perhaps the place to start is the standard Python Tutorial (http://docs.python.org/tutorial), though it is written more for a computer science audience rather than an AOS audience. Michael Williams's Handbook of the Physics Computing Course (http://pentangle.net/python/handbook) is a nice tutorial. Though it does not cover i/o and is geared for an audience of physicists, it is accessible to new Python users of all kinds. We've also listed a number of tutorials at PyAOS, both those that address Python for general science users (http://pyaos.johnny-lin.com/?page_id=215) and AOS-specific tutorials (http://pyaos.johnny-lin.com/?page_id=217).

Reference manuals: I really like *Python in a Nutshell* (Martelli, 2006). It's perhaps best known for providing a handy (but long) list of functions and options, but its explanations of key Python concepts, while terse, nonetheless are clear and illuminating. However, *Nutshell* is not a good resource for newbies; it assumes a formidable level of prior knowledge about computer science concepts.

The Python Language Reference (http://docs.python.org/reference) is the definitive guide to Python syntax, but I think its language and explanations are even farther removed from the world of non-computer scientists. I've found Martelli's descriptions and organization to be more helpful and understandable, as a result. The Python Standard Library (http://docs.python.org/library) documentation describes all the built-in functions and modules that

---

[3]For Matlab to Python, see http://www.scipy.org/NumPy_for_Matlab_Users. For IDL to Python, see https://www.cfa.harvard.edu/~jbattat/computer/python/science/idl-numpy.html. Both are accessed August 17, 2012.

come with Python. The os, sys, and unittest modules mentioned earlier are described here.

Finally, the NumPy and SciPy online documentation (http://docs.scipy.org/doc) is a must-bookmark site. Keep the NumPy list of functions in easy reach: http://www.scipy.org/Numpy_Functions_by_Category.

Other texts: It seems like everyday brings a new crop of books on Python, geared generally for data analysts and scientists. I haven't had the chance to look through most of these resources, so my recommendation to you would be to search a phrase like "python scientific programming" in your favorite bookseller's search engine.

10.4 A parting invitation

Throughout this book, I've mentioned the PyAOS website. As we end our time together, let me extend an invitation to you, gentle reader, to come and join PyAOS. Through our website, blog, and mailing list, we aim to support atmospheric and oceanic science users of Python: to help new users learn the language and experienced users to share with one other the cutting-edge work going on with the language. We're online at: http://pyaos.johnny-lin.com. Hope to see you there, soon! Lunch is on us ☺!

Come join PyAOS!

10.4. A PARTING INVITATION

Glossary

attribute data bound to an object that are designed to be acted on by methods also bound to that object.

calling execute or run a function.

class the template or "pattern" all instances of that class follow.

data coordinates a coordinate system for a plot where locations are specified by the values of the x- and y-axes data ranges.

delimit show where a sequence or collection begins and ends.

development environment an application that facilitates software development, often by providing coding, documentation, debugging, and execution tools in one place.

docstring a triple-quote delimited string that goes right after the `def` statement (or similar construct) and which provides a "help"-like description of the function.

dynamically typed variables take on the type of whatever value they are set to when they are assigned.

exception an error state in the program that cannot be processed by the current scope.

immutable a variable/object that cannot be changed.

import compile a module or package and make what is in the module or package accessible to the Python program that is doing the importing.

inherit incorporate the attribute and method definitions of another class into a definition of a new class of objects.

Glossary

inheritance dealing with inheriting attribute and method definitions of another class into a definition of a new class of objects.

instance an object that is the specific realization of a class of objects.

instantiate create an instance of a class.

instantiating creating an instance of a class.

instantiation the act of creating an instance of a class.

interpreter the execution environment for Python commands.

iterable a data structure that one can go through, one element at a time; in such a structure, after you've looked at one element of it, it will move you on to the next element.

iterator used nearly interchangably with the noun form of "iterable".

method functions bound to an object that are designed to act on the data also bound to that object.

module an importable Python source code file that typically contains function, class, and variable object definitions.

multi-paradigm language a computer language that supports multiple programming methodologies, for instance, object-oriented programming and procedural programming.

mutable a variable/object that can be changed.

namespace a set of function, variable, class, etc. names; these names can be stored inside an object variable and referenced via that variable.

newline character a special text code that specifies a new line; the specific code is operating system dependent.

object a "variable" that has attached to it both data (attributes) and functions designed to act on that data (methods).

object file for a compiled language, this is a file produced by the compiler after compiling the source code file; this is *not* an object in the sense of object-oriented programming.

package a directory of importable Python source code files (and, potentially, subpackages) that typically contains function, class, and variable object definitions.

package manager a program that streamlines the installation of tools and applications as part of an operating system or distribution; this is not to be confused with a Python package, which is not, in general, an operating system or distribution package.

procedural programming a programming paradigm where a program is broken up into discrete procedures or subroutines, each of which do a specified task and communicate with the rest of the program solely (ideally) through input and output variables that are passed in argument lists and/or return values..

PyAOS a web community whose goal is to support the use of Python in the atmospheric and oceanic sciences; see http://pyaos.johnny-lin.com.

rank the number of dimensions in an array; thus, a 2-D array has rank 2.

runtime when some code or a program is actually executing.

shape a tuple whose elements are the number of elements in each dimension of an array; in Python, the elements are arranged so the fastest varying dimension is the last element in the tuple and the slowest varying dimension is the first element in the tuple.

terminal window a text window in which you can directly type in operating system and other commands.

typecode a single character string that specifies the type of the elements of a NumPy array.

Glossary

Acronyms

AMS American Meteorological Society.

AOS atmospheric and oceanic sciences.

API application programming interface.

CDAT Climate Data Analysis Tools.

cdms Climate Data Management System.

CISL Computational Information Systems Laboratory.

dpi dots per inch.

EPD Enthought Python Distribution.

GCM general circulation model.

GUI graphical user interface.

HOPS Hyperslab OPerator Suite.

i/o input/output.

IDL Interactive Data Language.

LLNL Lawrence Livermore National Laboratory.

NCAR National Center for Atmospheric Research.

NGL NCAR Graphics Language.

NRCC Northeast Regional Climate Center.

Acronyms

OO object-oriented.

OOP object-oriented programming.

PCMDI Program for Coupled Model Diagnostics and Intercomparison.

UV-CDAT Ultrascale Visualization-Climate Data Analysis Tools.

vcs Visualization Control System.

Bibliography

Basili, V. R. and Selby, R. W. (1987). Comparing the effectiveness of software testing strategies. *IEEE Trans. Software Eng.*, SE-13(12):1278–1296.

Curtis, B. (1995). Objects of our desire: Empirical research on object-oriented development. *Human-Computer Interaction*, 10:337–344.

Lin, J. W.-B. (2009). qtcm 0.1.2: a Python implementation of the Neelin-Zeng Quasi-Equilibrium Tropical Circulation Model. *Geosci. Model Dev.*, 2:1–11, doi:10.5194/gmd–2–1–2009.

Lin, J. W.-B. (2012). Why Python is the next wave in earth sciences computing. *Bull. Amer. Meteor. Soc.*, (submitted).

Martelli, A. (2006). *Python in a Nutshell*. O'Reilly Media, Sebastopol, CA, 2nd edition.

BIBLIOGRAPHY

Index

`allclose`, 19
`append`, 24
`arange`, 49, 50
ArcGIS, 167
arguments, *see* parameters
`array`, 40, 48
arrays, **47**
    array syntax, 59, 60
    boolean, 65
    comparisons, 59, 64–71
    compatibility checking, 60
    converting types, 55
    creating, 47, 50, 55
    data types, **48**, 53, 55
    element ordering, 51
    flexible code, 54, 64
    help, 72
    indices, 50
    inquiry, **53**
    line continuation, 52
    looping through, 58
    loops vs. array syntax, 59
    multi-dimensional, 51
    operations, 58, 60, 69
    operators as functions, 60
    rank, 53, 60
    reshape, 54
    shape, 53
    size, 53, 54
    slicing, *see* slicing, 84
    subarrays, 53
    typecodes, *see* arrays, data types
assignment, 17, 74, 132, 140
    dictionary elements, 95
    list elements, 23, 26
    reference vs. value, 140
    using dictionaries for, 93
`assignValue`, 84
`astype`, 55, 77, 91, 102
`attrgetter`, 111
attributes, 41, 98, 138
    delete, 133
    get, 133
    inquiry, 133
    listing, 42
    private, 101
    public, 102
    setting, 133
`axis`, 158

backslash
    line continuation, 26
    string character, 19
`barbs`, 156
Basemap, 158
    coastlines, 160
    contour plots on a map, 159
    cylindrical projection, 160
    installing, 159
    latitude lines, 160
    longitude lines, 160
`boxfill`, 124

calculator, 14
`__call__`, 160
Callahan, Steven, 5
CapWords, 105

INDEX

case sensitivity, 18
CDAT, 78, 80, 167
`cdms2`, 124
`clabel`, 155, 157
clarity, 2
`class`, 98, 104
`close`, 74
`cm`, 155
`cmap`, 155
colons, 34
`colorbar`, 155, 158
`colors`, 155
command history, 12, 13
comment character, 62
commercial software, 7
common blocks, 118
`concatenate`, 55
continuation character, *see* backslash, line continuation
`contour`, 154, 158
contour plots, *see* matplotlib, contour plots
`contourf`, 155, 158
copy, 140
`correlate`, 71
`count`, 100
course files, viii, 9
`createDimension`, 84
`createVariable`, 84, 85
Ctrl-d, 10
`cumsum`, 103

data analysis, 89
    dynamic, 131
        missing values, 121
`deepcopy`, 140
`def`, 29, 63, 104
`delattr`, 132
delimiting code blocks, 30
development environments, 11
`__dict__`, 137

dictionaries, **26**, 93, 94, 137
    dynamically filling, 95
    flexible code, 95, 134
    keys, 27, 29
    methods, 27
    values, 27
`dir`, 11, 42, 99
directory listing, 93
`__doc__`, 101
docstrings, *see* documenting code
documenting code, 62, 166
    docstrings, 63
Doutriaux, Charles, 124, 125
Drach, Bob, 124, 125
`dtype`, 48, 53, 103
dynamically typed, *see* types, dynamic

`elif`, 34
`else`, 34
Enthought Python Distribution, 8
Epoch, 70
Epydoc, 166
`except`, 44
exceptions
    exception classes, 43, 45
    handling, 44, 165
    throwing, 43
`exp`, 71

f2py, 166
`False`, 20
`fft`, 71
`figure`, 150, 152
file input/output, 90
    close file objects, 74
    file objects, 74
    multiple-column text, 79
    netCDF, *see* netCDF
    open to append, 74
    open to read, 74
    open to write, 74

reading a text file, 75
single-column text, 77
writing to a text file, 75
`filled`, 128, 129
`fill_value`, 123, 128
Fiorino, Michael, 5
`float`, 76, 78
`fontsize`, 155
`for`, 34
free gift, ix
functional programming, 1
functions, **29**, 138
as objects, 94
calling, 138
parameters, *see* parameters
return values, 29, 62

`getattr`, 132, 138
`getValue`, 81
`glob`, 93
GNU/Linux, 8, 9
GRIB, 87

`hamming`, 71
`hasattr`, 132
`has_key`, 28
HDF, 87
hello world, 10, 12
`help`, 11, 72
`histogram`, 71
Hunter, John, 144

`id`, 141
IDL to Python, 168
IDLE, 12
`if`, 33, 64
`import`, 39
importing
aliasing, 41
data, 41
functions, 41
indentation, 29

inheritance, 106, 165, 166
`__init__`, 104, 106, 111
`insert`, 24
installing, **7**
`int`, 76, 95
`interp`, 71
interpreter, 10–11
exit, 10, 12
IPython, 11
`is`, 21
`isupper`, 100

`join`, 76

`keys`, 28
`kurtosis`, 96

`len`, 22, 38
`levels`, 154, 155
line plots, *see* matplotlib, line plots
`linesep`, 77
Linux, *see* GNU/Linux
lists, **22**, 137
complex references, 23
indices, 22, 23
initialize, 38
lengths, 22
looping through, 34
methods, 24
shuffling, 139
slicing, *see* slicing
logical testing, 33
compound tests, 33
`logical_and`, 65
`logical_not`, 69
`logical_or`, 65
looping, **34**
by indices, 35
iterators, 35

`ma`, 40, 126
Mac OS X, 9

INDEX

__main__, 112
map projections, *see* Basemap
masked arrays, 40, **122**, 126–130
    converting to an array, 128
    creating, 126, 127
    fill values, 123, 128
    masks, 123, 129
    operations, 123, 130
masked variables, **122**, 124
    creating, 126
masked_array, 126
masked_greater, 127
masked_where, 127
Matlab to Python, 168
matplotlib, 143
    axis labeling, 153
    Basemap, *see* Basemap
    color bars, 155
    color maps, 155
    colors, 145, 149
    contour levels, 154
    contour plots, 154
    contour plots on a map, 159
    displaying vs. saving figures, 152
    filled contour plots, 155
    line and marker property listings, 146
    line plots, 144
    lined and filled contour plot, 155
    linestyle, 145, 147
    linewidth, 145
    map projections, *see* Basemap
    markers, 145, 148
    multiple curves on one figure, 151
    multiple independent figures, 150
    negative contours dashed, 155
    pyplot, 144
    save figure, 152, 154
    save figure then visualize, 154
    save figure without displaying, 147, 154
    using LaTeX to annotate plots, 146
    visualizing plots, 144
    wind barbs, 156
max, 42
mean, 90
median, 90
meshgrid, 56, 117, 156
methods, 41, 98, 99, 138
    calling, 100, 102
    defining, 104, 109
    delete, 133
    get, 133
    inquiry, 133
    listing, 42
    private, 101
    public, 102
    setting, 133
min, 42
missing values, *see* data analysis, missing values; masked arrays
modeling, 137, 141
modules, **39**
    importing, 39, 40
    submodules, 40

__name__, 112
namespaces, 2, 40
    module names vs. namespaces, 41
    preventing collisions, 41, 94
netCDF
    creating dimensions, 84
    creating variable objects, 84
    dimensions, 80, 81
    file objects, 81
    filling array variables, 84
    filling scalar variables, 84
    global attributes, 80, 83
    metadata, 82
    reading a variable, 81

structure, 80
unlimited dimension, 83
variables, 80, 81
newline character, 19, 75, 77, 78
`nlevels`, 154
`None`, 21
Noon, William, 6
NumPy, *see also* arrays, 40, **47**, 126
importing, 47, 49, 126

`object`, 106
object-oriented programming, 97–99
vs. procedural, 113, 115, 119, 120, 137
objects, 110
attributes, *see* attributes
calling, 160
classes, 98, 104, 110
inheritance, *see* inheritance
instances, 98, 106, 110
instantiation, 104, 116, 134
listing attributes and methods, 42, 99
methods, *see* methods
programming, *see* object-oriented programming
syntax, 41, 100
open, 74, 90
OpenDAP, 167
operators
addition, 18
defining, 101
division, 15, 18, 19
equal, 18, 21
exponentiation, 18
greater than, 18
greater than or equal to, 18
`is`, 21
less than, 18
less than or equal to, 18
logical, 20

multiplication, 18
not equal, 18
subtraction, 18
ordinal value, 22
`orientation`, 155
os, 77, 166
paths, 166

package manager, 8
packages, *see* modules
pandas, 167
parameters
functions, 29, 30
initialize, 22, 31, 134
keyword, 30
passing in lists of arguments, 32
positional, 30
ParaView, 162
`pass`, 64
`permutations`, 139
platform independence, 1, 77, 166
`plot`, 144
potential temperature, 62
`print`, 14, 19, 102
procedural programming, 98
vs. object-oriented, 113, 115, 119, 120
programming
dynamic subroutine management, 137
dynamic variable management, 131, 133
provenance management, 3
PyAOS, 169
PyGrADS, 162, 167
PyNGL, 78, 143, 162, 167
PyNIO, 80, 87, 167
pyplot, *see* matplotlib, pyplot
pysclint, 80, 87
PyTables, 73, 80, 87
pytest, 166

INDEX

Python(x,y), 11
PYTHONPATH, 41
PyUnit, *see* unittest

`raise`, 43
`range`, 35
`rank`, 53
`ravel`, 55, 103
`readline`, 75
`readlines`, 75, 79
reference manuals, 168
`remove`, 24
`repeat`, 55
`reshape`, 54, 103
`resize`, 103
reStructuredText, 63
`return`, 29, 62
`reverse`, 42
`round`, 103
RPy, 167
runlist, 137

SAGE, 167
Saravanan, R., 136
`savefig`, 152, 154, 158
ScientificPython, 80
    importing, 80
SciPy, 160, 165, 167
    importing, 165
scripting, 1
`self`, 104, 107, 110
`setattr`, 107, 132
`shape`, 53, 102
`show`, 144, 158
`sin`, 40, 71
`size`, 53
`skew`, 96
slicing
    arrays, 50, 53
    lists, 23
    strings, 25

`sorted`, 28, 111, 112
sorting, 93, 112
Sphinx, 63, 166
`split`, 76
Spyder, 11
`std`, 90
strings, 19
    attributes, 99
    concatenation, 20, 76, 114
    converting, 76
    methods, 99
    splitting, 76
    triple quotes, 20
style guide, 46
`subplot`, 156
sys, 166
    search path, 166

T, 102, 103
tab character, 19, 76, 79
terminal window, 11
testing, 112, 166
`time`, 70
timings, 70
`title`, 99
Tk, 12
transpose, 103
`transpose`, 55, 102
`True`, 20
`try`, 44
tutorials, 168
typecodes, *see* arrays, data types
types
    arrays, *see* arrays
    basic, 17
    booleans, 20
    dictionaries, *see* dictionaries
    dynamic, 17, 22, 35, 92
    floating, 19
    integers, 19
    lists, *see* lists

NoneType, 21
strings, *see* strings
tuples, 25
upcasting, 19

underscore, *see* attributes, private; methods, private
unittest, 112, 166
`upper`, 99, 100
UV-CDAT, *see also* CDAT; cdms2, 80, 87, 124, 162, 167

`ValueError`, 43, 44
`values`, 28
vcs, 124, 143
VisTrails, 162
visualization, 143, 162
VPython, 163

weather maps, 3
`where`, 66, 67
`while`, 36
widgets, 12
Williams, Dean, 124, 125
Windows, 8
`write`, 75
`writelines`, 75
WxMAP2, 3

`xrange`, 59

`zeros`, 49

INDEX

About the Author

Johnny Wei-Bing Lin graduated from Stanford University with a B.S. in Mechanical Engineering and an M.S. in Civil Engineering-Water Resources. After working as an environmental engineer, he returned to school and received his Ph.D. in Atmospheric Sciences from UCLA. His atmospheric sciences research is focused on stochastic convective parameterizations, ice-atmosphere interactions in the Arctic, and simple frameworks for modularizing climate models. He has chaired the AMS Python Symposiums and has taught or co-taught some of the AMS Python short courses. Johnny also helps coordinate the PyAOS mailing list and blog (http://pyaos.johnny-lin.com), an effort at building up the atmospheric and oceanic sciences Python community. Currently, he is a Professor of Physics at North Park University in Chicago.

Colophon

This book was written using PDFLaTeX (PDFTeX 3.1415926-1.40.10-2.2) and the Vim editor, running on an Ubuntu 12.04 GNU/Linux system. Times-like fonts are provided by the TX Fonts package (http://www.ctan.org/pkg/txfonts). The title page and examples environment are based on the "titleTMB" example from Peter Wilson's July 13, 2010 work *Some Examples of Title Pages* (http://www.ctan.org/tex-archive/info/latex-samples/TitlePages).

Special Gift for Print Copy Owners

The original owners of a print copy of this book can download a copy of the latest edition of the Full PDF version of the book (the one with hyperlinks enabled) at http://www.johnny-lin.com/pyintro/gift.shtml. When prompted, please enter in "ihaveaprintcopy" for the username and "AOSPython2012" for the password. (Both username and password are all one word with no punctuation marks. Notice in the password the second character is a letter while the second-to-last character is a numeral.) Thanks for purchasing a print copy of the book!

www.ingramcontent.com/pod-product-compliance
Lightning Source LLC
Chambersburg PA
CBHW080909170526
45158CB00008B/2055